# The Book of the General Lawes and Libertyes Concerning the Inhabitants of the Massachusets

*Reproduced in facsimile from the unique 1648 edition in the Huntington Library*

*Edited with an Introduction by* Thomas G. Barnes

THE HUNTINGTON LIBRARY, SAN MARINO, CALIFORNIA. 1975

ISBN 0-87328-066-0

Library of Congress Catalog Number 75-12004

Copyright © 1975

Henry E. Huntington Library and Art Gallery

Designed and printed by Grant Dahlstrom at the Castle Press, Pasadena, California

# Introduction

"It is ordered, by the full Courte, that the bookes of lawes, now at the presse, may be sould in quires, at three shillings the booke; provided that every member of this Courte shall have one without price, & the auditor generall, & Mr. Joseph Hill, for which there shalbe 50 in all so disposed, by appointment of this Courte."[1]

With this order of 27 October 1648, the General Court of Massachusetts concluded its three years' continuous involvement with the enactment and preparation of *The Book of the General Lawes and Libertyes Concerning the Inhabitants of the Massachusets.*[2] The *Lawes and Libertyes* was a remarkable achievement. It served as the model for subsequent compilations of statute law in Massachusetts and had great influence on the beginning of printed law in other New England colonies.

The agitation for such a compendium of the colony's laws began in 1635 when the freemen's deputies sought positive laws by which the discretion of magistrates would be both bounded and limited. The first of a succession of committees "for the laws"— comprising Governor John Haynes, Deputy-Governor Richard Bellingham, John Winthrop, and Thomas Dudley — was appointed by the General Court, 6 May 1635, to "make a draught of such lawes as they shall iudge needefull for the well ordering of this plantacion, & to present the same to the Court."[3] The reluctance of the magistrates to allow limitation of their discretion in judicial matters caused this and subsequent committees prior to 1645 to do their work in what was at best a half-hearted manner. The sole fruit of the early committees was the "Body of Liberties" of 1641. This was a major and lasting contribution to the "laws," but it failed to limit sufficiently the magistrates' discretion, and consequently failed to quiet the rising clamor for a comprehensive, printed collection of the positive law of the colony. Only

with the appointment of three county committees (for Suffolk, Middlesex, and Essex counties), on 1 July 1645, each "chosen to draw up a body of laws and present them to the consideration of the General Court at their next sitting,"[4] was the first effectual step taken toward printing the laws. On these committees for the first time the non-magistrate element (clergy and deputies) outnumbered the magistrate. The committee of 22 May 1646, charged with drawing together the county committees' drafts and with examining the "abbreviation of the laws in force" prepared by its leading magistrate, Richard Bellingham, comprised two magistrates, two deputies, and one minister.[5] Subsequent committees did not again see such non-magistrate majorities. However, sufficient was the public clamor, the effective and tireless labor of the principal deputy member, Joseph Hills (rightly named to receive a free copy of the printed laws), that the labors of these later committees for the laws resulted in massive legislation over two years and the compiling and publishing of most of the colony's general statutory law in the *Lawes and Libertyes* of 1648. Reinforcing public clamor and Hills's devotion was the magistrates' recognition of the benefit of printed laws to themselves in the performance of their judicial duties.

Without the conversion of the magistrates, sitting as the governor and assistants in the upper house of the General Court, to the proposition that the printing of the laws was advantageous, the 1648 book would not have been. Conversion is not too strong a word; and like most conversions, that of the magistrates was in part gradual and in part sudden. Some magistrates, particularly men like Richard Bellingham, who had been a barrister in England, were sympathetic to the idea of explicitly stating fundamental "laws." The "Body of Liberties" of 1641 was such a statement and one

5

that persisted. More significantly, the magistrates, as the upper house of the General Court, were not afraid to legislate, to make "laws" or to promulgate orders so wide in scope as to constitute legislation. Over the course of the first fifteen years of the colony's existence the amount of legislation increased steadily. There were false starts — enactments tried, deemed to have failed, then repealed — and there were tentative enactments set forth for a limited period, usually as a necessary expedient to deal with a pressing immediate problem. But overall, the records of the General Court grew increasingly more ponderous with "laws." Consequently, the magistrates acting either alone or collectively in the Quarterly Courts of Assistants became increasingly unsure of what was, and what was not, the law of Massachusetts. This was particularly the case in the realm of criminal and public law. For the civil law (the law governing actions between party-and-party) the common law of England provided sufficient guidance and much of the substance as well as most of the procedure implemented in the Massachusetts courts. In the realm of criminal law, the magistrates had strong notions as to the nature of a "Godly commonwealth" which urged them to be both innovative and less bound to the structure and penalties of English criminal law. Their individuality was strengthened by their familiarity with the old English criminal law of felonies and its uniform punishment by hanging, which they considered too unmeasured in its severity. They were further influenced by the realization that the most serious threat of disorder to society came in those more sophisticated crimes that corrupted justice, raised the specter of insurrection, oppressed and defrauded the citizen: these include sedition, slander, contempt of magistrates, perjury, vexatious litigation, fraud, forgery, extortion, subornation.[6] The ideal of a "Godly commonwealth" also prompted the Massachusetts magistrates to simplify the archaic English law of property and property rights and the confused mass of English statute law that supposedly regulated trade and manufacturing, provided for taxes, and governed the outward manifestation of im-

morality (as distinct from simple criminality). By the early 1640s, so far had the magistrates in the General Court gone towards the establishment of their "Godly commonwealth" both by legislation and by judicial practice that there was marked advantage to be gained by them in the gathering and rationalization of the "laws."

The sudden part of the magistrates' conversion was the realization that the clamor for printed laws could not be stilled. The freemen's elected deputies, meeting separately from the magistrates in the House of Deputies of the General Court, had begun to take on the attributes of a settled branch of government: continuity of experience, increasing expertise in procedure, a platform from which to express and a power base from which to press for their interests, and evolution of a recognized leadership within the House. The conversion was completed in November 1646, when Dr. Robert Child and his six very substantial supporters petitioned the General Court for "civil liberty and freedom" for non-churchmen and the enlargement of membership in the church. The Court responded with a dozen charges against the "remonstrants" (which resulted in their trial and punishment), the fifth of which was that they "goe about to weaken the authority of our lawes, . . . by perswading the people, through want of the body of English lawes, & partly through the insufficyency or ill frame of those wee have, they cann expect no sure enjoyment of their lives & libertyes vnder them."[7] Perhaps it was coincidence that this same session of the General Court, 4 November 1646, saw the passage of the first large segment of new laws that appear to have grown from the work of the committee for the laws. It was probably not coincidence that for the first time the governor and assistants came out foursquare for printed laws in a general order of that session, "so as we may have ready recourse to any of them [the laws] upon all occasions, whereby we may manifest our utter disaffection to arbitrary government, & so all relations be safely & sweetly directed & perfected in all their iust rights & priviledges . . . ."[8] Dr. Child was the most serious threat the colony had faced in a challenge to its basic polity, juridical integrity, and legislative autonomy. The threat was not lost on the magistrates.

It is now customary to refer to *The Book of the General Lawes and Libertyes* as the "Code of 1648." The most recent and most persuasive authority on the nature of early colonial law in Massachusetts, Professor George Lee Haskins, describes the *Lawes and Libertyes* as

a comprehensive legal code which was an authoritative compilation not only of constitutional guarantees, provisions for the conduct of government, trade, military affairs, and the relations between church and state, but of the substantive law of crime, tort, property, domestic relations. The Code was no mere collection of English laws and customs, but was a fresh and considered effort to order men's lives and conduct in accordance with the religious and political ideals of Puritanism.[9]

There is a touch of overstatement in this description. In subsequent chapters of his work, Professor Haskins corrects an oft-distorted view of early Massachusetts law by giving due credit to the importance of English laws and customs in the colony and by reducing to reasonable proportions the Puritan contribution to the colony's early law-making and law-doing efforts. More particularly, there is only modest provision in the Book concerning the substantive law of crime: capital crimes, manslaughter, larceny, fraud, forgery, contempt, heresy, and barratry along with laws in restraint of immorality are the principal heads represented and do not constitute the full extent of the criminal law as enforced in the colony's courts. Tort hardly figures at all, and is most prominent in provisions concerning trespassing beasts, fences, etc. Property is limited largely to very general provisions of which the most important concern the security of property by record, dowries, escheat for want of heir, prohibition of feudal incidents, intestacy, wrecks, and intertidal rights. Domestic relations are rather more complete. It is clear, however, from even the most cursory examination of the records of judicial proceedings, at first instance, that there existed a large and flourishing body of law in each of the

areas (domestic relations excepted) about which the Book is silent.[10] It is in the realm of "constitutional guarantees, provisions for the conduct of government, trade, military affairs, and the relations between church and state" along with procedural law that the *Lawes and Libertyes* is most comprehensive and definitive in the matter of judicial practice.

The fact that so much of the law in force in Massachusetts was not based on the Book would not necessarily rob it of the pretentious title of "code" in the rather loose American use of the term.[11] What makes it something less than a code is the fact that not all of the legislation of the General Court in force at the time of publication was considered to be contained in the *Lawes and Libertyes*. The dedicatory epistle itself indicates the limitation: "For such lawes and orders as are not of generall concernment we have not put them into this booke, but they remain still in force, and are to be seen in the booke of the Records of the Court, but all generall laws not heer inserted nor mentioned to be still of force are to be accounted repealed." The General Court was not clear as to what was meant by "generall concernment." At the 11 November 1647 session of the Court that confirmed the last major segments of the committee's revisions for inclusion in the Book, at least one law of "generall concernment" was passed that was not included in the Book: an order requiring written pleadings in civil actions.[12] It was such a law as this that the Court referred to on 18 October 1648 when it ordered "That all lawes, orders, & acts of Courte, contained in the ould bookes, that are of force, & not ordered to be printed. . . ." be transcribed in an alphabetical arrangement.[13] It is not to disparage the work of the committees for the laws to see their efforts as essentially statute law revision rather than codification, in which even the revision did not pretend to comprehensiveness.

There *was* a "code" of laws enacted for Massachusetts in the early colonial period: the "Body of Liberties" of 1641. The work of the Rev. Nathaniel Ward, onetime barrister of Lincoln's Inn, this was a code even in the Romano-Civil Law tradition, setting out fundamental legal principles by rational categories:[14]

Preamble (first paragraph of which included as preamble to *The Lawes and Libertyes*, p. 1)
clauses 1-17: general civil liberties
18-57: "Rites Rules and Liberties concerning Juditiall proceedings"
58-78: "Liberties more peculiarlie concerning the free men"
79-80: "Liberties of Woemen"
81-84: "Liberties of Children"
85-88: "Liberties of Servants"
89-91: "Liberties of Forreiners and Strangers"
92-93: protection of "Bruite Creatures"
94: "Capitall Lawes" (12 subsections)
95: "A Declaration of the Liberties of the Lord Jesus hath given to the Churches" (11 subsections)
96-98: enabling, empowering, amending, sanctions, etc.
Final clause: questions requiring interpretation, etc.

Of these one hundred clauses only fourteen are not found in the *Lawes and Libertyes*, and four of those omitted are the expired clauses 96-98 and final clause.[15] The eighty-six clauses (almost all wholly unaltered) that are in the 1648 book are scattered throughout it, no more subtly categorized than the crude alphabetical heads by which the *Lawes and Libertyes* was arranged by the committees for the laws. This chopping up was the measure of how little the later committees were concerned with the ends and methodology of codification. There was no reason why they should be concerned — the public clamor and the magistrates' own needs were not for a "code" (the "Body of Liberties" would have sufficed) but for a book of statutes.

The models for the committees' book appear to have been three types of current English legal literature well known to most of the magistrates and certainly to those with legal training: 1) abridgments of statutes and compilations of statutes at large; 2) lawyers' commonplace books comprising extracts from statutes, Year Books, reports, treatises, formu-

laries, and oddments such as maxims from civilians, Canonists, and the Fathers; 3) practice books, particularly handbooks for justices of the peace and court keepers. Joseph Hills, the prominent deputy member of the committees, had thoroughly perused Ferdinando Pulton's *Collection of Sundrie Statutes Frequent in Use*, which was arranged chronologically with a "kalendar" of the acts under alphabetical titles.[16] The *Lawes and Libertyes* bears a striking resemblance to Michael Dalton's *Countrey Justice*, the currently most popular handbook for English justices of the peace, which was largely arranged by alphabetical headings of various categories of crimes and of the concerns of the justices.[17] The prominent Massachusetts magistrate William Pynchon of Springfield approved of Dalton as a sound guide, and Dalton's book was one of six works, two copies of each of which were to be purchased for the General Court's use by order of 11 of November 1647.[18] The alphabetical arrangement of the *Lawes and Libertyes* was apparently chosen to facilitate its use by magistrates, clerks, and also attorneys. Such an arrangement was dictated more by the requirements of a professional readership than of a lay or popular readership.

How much of the *Lawes and Libertyes* represented previously enacted laws and how much was the work of the committees for the laws? The List of Entries and Sources of "Laws" which is appended to this edition provides an answer. About two-thirds of the provisions in the printed book were based upon enactments of the General Court between 1630 and 1645 — including "The Body of Liberties" — and the rest were enacted between 1646 and 1648 and were presumably the work of the later committees.[19] As the List indicates, the later committees did considerable rearranging of previously enacted laws, making a number of emendations and additions to them and deleting other portions. The later committees aimed at a thorough rationalization of the colony's statute law, both in existing law and by means of the new law which they drafted. The *Lawes and Libertyes* was a very successful essay in rational statute law revision.

The dedicatory epistle, "To our beloved

brethren and neighbours," is of interest if for no other reason than that it contains a major part of the explicitly Biblically-derived text that is to be found in the *Lawes and Libertyes*. Only in the section on "Capital Lawes" (pages 5-6) are citations given to the Bible for provisions in the law; the committees appear to have deleted a reference to Exodus 22:2 in the section on "Man-slaughter" (page 37) which was in the original law enacted by the General Court.[20] Professor Haskins has put the matter of the Massachusetts founders' dependence on the Bible as a source of law in proper perspective and has effectively demolished the older (and erroneous) interpretation which argued that a "Godly commonwealth" meant a "Biblical commonwealth." Professor Haskins conjectures that the author of the epistle was John Winthrop.[21] In part his conjecture is based on Winthrop's known views on the nature of law (a human creation based upon natural law) as against a variant, even more Puritan, notion of law espoused by the Rev. John Cotton: that law must be based on "explicit divine precepts."[22] Cotton's view had been expressed in "Moses his Judicials," which Cotton had drawn up in 1636 as a proposed body of laws to answer the growing demand for printed laws; this work is referred to in the last paragraph of the first page of the epistle. Cotton's endeavor was a competitor to Ward's "Body of Liberties," but as the epistle rightly indicates, it lost the race to Ward in 1641. What is ironic and hitherto unnoticed is the fact that the Biblical references in the epistle to the *Lawes and Libertyes* owe much to none other than the Rev. John Cotton. In an undated letter from Cotton to Winthrop, Cotton recommends wording that constitutes the second and third sentences of the text of the epistle, but includes citations to the Old Testament which are omitted in the epistle.[23] More significantly, the entire last paragraph of the epistle is Cotton's work, virtually verbatim from his letter to Winthrop. Here, the references are to St. Paul's Epistle to the Romans; they reflect the Pauline emphasis in the first paragraph of the dedicatory epistle which does not appear to have been Cotton's contribution. The distinction between John Winthrop's Pauline theology — assuming he in fact drafted the epistle and incorporated Cotton's contribution in the last paragraph with its citations to Romans — and Cotton's Old Testament foundation is the clearest indicator of the two men's differing approaches to the relationship between law and Biblical authority. Winthrop (and St. Paul) have the first word on the title page: "Whosoever therefore resisteth the power, resisteth the ordinance of God, and they that resist receive to themselves damnation. Romanes 13.2." Both have the last word, too, in the nature of the *Lawes and Libertyes*.

The *Lawes and Libertyes* was a remarkable achievement. It stilled the clamor for printed laws. It provided an essential tool for the increasingly sophisticated (and increasingly professional) implementation of the law in the practice of the courts in Massachusetts. It had great influence on the beginning of printed law in other New England colonies. It was an important model for the colonists' coreligionists in England who sought — albeit without success — the reform of English law in the brief summer of Cromwell's "Godly commonwealth."[24] It served as the model for subsequent compilations of statute law in Massachusetts. To borrow the Civil Law aphorism that the dedicatory epistle uses to justify the making of law, *"Crescit in Orbe dolus"*: indeed evil does grow in the world, but known and established laws such as those set forth in the *Lawes and Libertyes* of 1648 provided a foundation not only for the punishment of malefactors but for the preservation of civil liberties. Those two sides of the same coin, the law, have been a fundamental element in the development of this country.

\* \* \* \* \* \*

The *Lawes and Libertyes* was printed with a table at the end which, to judge by the 1660 revision of the *Lawes and Libertyes*, was something more than a table of contents but not much of an index.[25] The Huntington's unique copy of the 1648 book lacks the table. The apparatus appended to this edition provides the "generall Titles and chief Heads," which the original table would have given, along with an indication of the sources of the various laws. Consequently, it is both a table of contents to the *Lawes and Libertyes* and an invitation to further research.

Even the most casual reader who uses this book should read George Lee Haskins, *Law and Authority in Early Massachusetts: A Study in Tradition and Design* (New York, 1960) in order to fit the *Lawes and Libertyes* into the context of early Massachusetts legal development. Further references for study can be derived from his very full notes.

## NOTES TO THE INTRODUCTION

[1] N.B. Shurtleff, ed., *Records of the Governor and Company of the Massachusetts Bay* (Boston, 1853), vol. 2, p. 262 hereafter, Mass. Rec. vol.: page. The auditor general was Nathaniel Duncan. It has been established that 600 copies were printed (William H. Whitmore, ed., *The Colonial Laws of Massachusetts* [Boston, 1889], p. 95 *n*57). The Huntington Library's copy is the only known survivor.

[2] The title page indicates publication was authorized by the General Court 14 March "1647" — 1648 in our reckoning. No explicit order of authorization is extant. However, an order of that session referred to the "speedy committing of them [amendments to the book passed] to the press . . ." (Mass. Rec. 2:227). By 10 May 1648 the book was "now at press" (Mass. Rec. 2:246). An amendment s.v. "Appeale" (p. 2) that was apparently ordered by the house of Deputies, 13 May 1648, and the upper house, 27 October 1648, was *not* made in the Huntington's unique copy (Mass. Rec. 2:263 and 3:130).

[3] Mass. Rec. 1:147.

[4] Mass. Rec. 3:26. This order is extant only in the Deputies' records. It is likely that the Deputies were the movers of this new departure.

[5] Mass. Rec. 2:157.

[6] I have dealt with this concern at greater length in "Law and Liberty (and Order) in Early Massachusetts," Clark Library Seminar Paper, 3 November 1973, which is in press.

[7] Mass. Rec. 3:90.

[8] Mass. Rec. 2:169.

[9] G. L. Haskins, *Law and Authority in Early Massachusetts* (New York, 1960), p. 2.

[10] See besides Court of Assistants records in Mass. Rec. 1, also John Noble, ed., *Records of the Courts of Assistants* (Boston, 1904), vol. II (1630-44) and J. F. Cronin, ed., (Boston, 1928), vol. III (1642-73); *Records and Files of the Quarterly Courts of Essex County* (Salem, 1911), vol. I (1636-56).

[11] The distinction between American use of "code" and the traditional idea of code in the Romano-Civil Law is succinctly put in René David & J.E.C. Brierly, *Major Legal Systems in the World Today* (London, 1968), pp. 380-81.

[12] Mass. Rec. 2:219.

[13] Mass. Rec. 2:260.

[14] Whitmore, pp. 29-64. The "Body of Liberties" was given force of law at the 10 December 1641 session of the General Court, Mass. Rec. 1:346.

[15] Omitted "Liberties," clauses: 14 (conveyances by married women, children, insane), 26 (unpaid attorneys), 27 (written pleas), 39 (respite of execution in civil suits), 50 (town choice of jurors), 51 (town election of associates), 55 (pleadings), 79 (widow's rights under intestacy), 80 (conjugal correction of wives).

[16] First edition, 1618 (STC 9328) and subsequent editions to 1661.

[17] First edition, 1618 (STC 6205) and fourteen more editions to 1697. Dalton also provides precedents, forms of warrants, etc., in the last chapters of his work, similar to pp. 55-59 of the *Lawes and Libertyes*.

[18] *Winthrop Papers*, vol. 4 (Boston, 1947), p. 135; Mass. Rec. 2:212.

[19] Based upon tabulation of the identified sources, 71% of the provisions were based upon enactments of the General Court, 1630-1645 (of which just under half were from "The Body of Liberties"), and 29% were enacted between 1646 and 1648 and were presumably the work of the later committees. If it is assumed that the "Not Found" and "Established Practice" sources were in fact the work of these later committees, then 63% were 1630-1645 enactments and 37% the work of later committees. My analysis agrees closely with Haskins, p. 136. The later committees were certainly responsible for the bulk of the 92 new provisions passed between 6 May 1646 and 11 November 1647 by the General Court. Three of their provisions (concerning county courts) date from March and May 1648 (p. 15, s.v. "Courts"), and a fourth concerning customs (p. 27, s.v. "Impost"), were passed by the General Court 10 May 1648. Since the amendment s.v. "Appeale" also dated from May 1648 but was *not* executed in the printing, it is possible that the four known 1648 provisions were merely given post facto confirmation by the Court; see note 2.

[20] See note 14 to List of Entries and Sources of "Laws."

[21] Haskins, p. 140.

[22] Haskins, pp. 159-60.

[23] *Winthrop Papers*, vol. 5 (Boston, 1947), pp. 192-93.

[24] Haskins, pp. 191-92.

[25] Whitmore, pp. 209-16.

# The Lawes and Libertyes

*THE*
BOOK OF THE GENERAL
## LAUUES AND LIBERTYES
CONCERNING THE INHABITANTS OF THE MASSACHUSETS
COLLECTED OUT OF THE RECORDS OF THE GENERAL COURT
FOR THE SEVERAL YEARS WHERIN THEY WERE MADE
AND ESTABLISHED,

And now revised by the same Court and disposed into an Alphabetical order
and published by the same Authorit.e in the General Court
held at *Boston* the fourteenth of the
first month *Anno*
1647.

---

*Whosoever therefore resisteth the power, resisteth the ordinance of God,
and they that resist receive to themselves damnation.* Romanes 13. 2.

---

---

*CAMBRIDGE.*
Printed according to order of the GENERAL COURT.
1648,

---

And are to be solde at the shop of *Hezekiah Usher*
in *Boston*

## TO OUR BELOVED BRETHREN AND NEIGHBOURS
the Inhabitants of the Massachuset, the Governour, Assistants
and Deputies assembled in the Generall Court of that
Jurisdiction with grace and peace in our
Lord Jesus Christ.

SO soon as God had set up Politicall Government among his people Israel hee gave
them a body of lawes for judgement both in civil and criminal causes. These were
breif and fundamental principles, yet withall so full and comprehensive as out of
them clear deductions were to be drawne to all particular cases in future times.
For a Common-wealth without lawes is like a Ship without rigging and steeradge. Nor is it
sufficient to have principles or fundamentals, but these are to be drawn out into so many of their
deductions as the time and condition of that people may have use of. And it is very unsafe &
injurious to the body of the people to put them to learn their duty and libertie from generall rule,
nor is it enough to have lawes except they be also just. Therefore among other priviledges
which the Lord bestowed upon his peculiar people, these he calls them specially to consider of, that
God was nearer to them and their lawes were more righteous then other nations. God was sayd
to be amongst them or neer to them because of his Ordinances established by himselfe. and their
lawes righteous because himselfe was their Law-giver: yet in the comparison are implyed two
things, first that other nations had somthing of Gods presence amongst them. Secondly that
there was also somwhat of equitie in their lawes, for it pleased the Father (upon the Covenant of
Redemption with his Son) to restore so much of his Image to lost man as whereby all nations are
disposed to worship God, and to advance righteousnes: which appears in that of the Apostle
Rom. 1. 21. They knew God &c: and in the 2. 14 They did by nature the things
conteined in the law of God. But the nations corrupting his Ordinances (both of Religion,
and Justice) God withdrew his presence from them proportionably whereby they were given up
to abominable lusts Rom. 2. 21. Whereas if they had walked according to that light & law
of nature they might have been preserved from such moral evils and might have injoyed a common blessing in all their natural and civil Ordinances: now, if it might have been so with the
nations who were so much strangers to the Covenant of Grace, what advantage bare they who
have interest in this Covenant, and may injoye the speciall presence of God in the puritie and native simplicitie of all his Ordinances by which he is so neer to his owne people. This hath been
no small priviledge, and advantage to us in New-England that our Churches, and civil State
have been planted, and growne up (like two twinnes) together like that of Israel in the wilder-
nes by which wee were put in minde (and had opportunitie put into our hands) not only to gather
our Churches, and set up the Ordinances of Christ Jesus in them according to the Apostolick
patterne by such light as the Lord graciously afforded us: but also withall to frame our civil Politie, and lawes according to the rules of his most holy word whereby each do helpe and strengthen
other (the Churches the civil Authoritie, and the civil Authoritie the Churches) and so both
prosper the better without such emulation, and contention for priviledges or prioritie as have
proved the misery (if not ruine) of both in some other places.

For this end about nine years since wee used the help of some of the Elders of our Churches
to compose a modell of the Judiciall lawes of Moses with such other cases as might be referred to
them, with intent to make use of them in composing our lawes, but not to have them published
as the lawes of this Jurisdiction: nor were they voted in Court. For that book intitled The
Liberties &c: published about seven years since (which conteines also many lawes and orders
both for civil & criminal causes, and is commonly (though without ground) reported to be our
Fundamentalls that wee owne as established by Authoritie of this Court, and that after three
years experience & generall probation: and accordingly we have inserted them into this volume under the severall heads to which they belong yet not as fundamentalls, for divers of them
have since been repealed, or altered, and more may justly be (at least) amended heerafter, as further experience shall discover defects or inconveniences for N.h.l simul natum et perfectum.

A 2.

The same must we say of this present Volume, we have not published it as a perfect body of lawes sufficient to carry on the Government established for future time, nor could it be expected that we should promise such a thing. For if it be no disparagement to the wisdome of that High Court of Parliament in England that in four hundred years they could not so compile their lawes, and regulate proceedings in Courts of justice &c: but that they had still new work to do of the same kinde almost every Parliament: there can be no just cause to blame a poor Colonie (being unfurnished of Lawyers and Statesmen) that in eighteen years hath produced no more, nor better rules for a good, and setled Government then this Book holds forth. nor have you (our Bretheren and Neighbours) any cause, whether you look back upon our Native Country, or take your observation by other States, & Common wealths in Europe) to complaine of such as you have imployed in this service; for the time which hath been spent in making lawes, and repealing and altering them so often, nor of the charge which the Country hath been put to for those occasions, the Civilian gives you a satisfactorie reason of such continuall alterations additions &c: Crescit in Orbe dolus.

These Lawes which were made successively in divers former years, we have reduced under severall heads in an alphabeticall method, that so they might the more readilye be found, & that the divers lawes concerning one matter being placed together the scope and intent of the whole and of every of them might the more easily be apprehended: we must confesse we have not been so exact in placing every law under its most proper title as we might, and would have been: the reason was our hasty indeavour to satisfie your longing expectation, and frequent complaints for want of such a volume to be published in print: wherin (upon every occasion) you might readily see the rule which you ought to walke by. And in this (we hope) you will finde satisfaction, by the help of the references under the severall heads, and the Table which we have added in the end. For such lawes and orders as are not of generall concernment we have not put them into this booke, but they remain still in force, and are to be seen in the booke of the Records of the Court, but all generall laws not heer inserted nor mentioned to be still of force are to be accounted repealed.

You have called us from amongst the rest of our Bretheren and given us power to make these lawes: we must now call upon you to see them executed: remembring that old & true proverb, The execution of the law is the life of the law. If one sort of you viz: non-Freemen should object that you had no hand in calling us to this worke, and therfore think your selvs not bound to obedience &c. Wee answer that a subsequent, or implicit consent is of like force in this case, as an expresse precedent power: for in putting your persons and estates into the protection and way of subsistance held forth and exercised within this Jurisdiction, you doe tacitly submit to this Government and to all the wholesome lawes therof, and so is the common repute in all nations and that upon this Maxim. Qui sentit commodum sentire debet et onus.

If any of you meet with some law that seemes not to tend to your particular benefit, you must consider that lawes are made with respect to the whole people, and not to each particular person: and obedience to them must be yeilded with respect to the common welfare, not to thy private advantage, and as thou yeildest obedience to the law for common good, but to thy disadvantage: so another must observe some other law for thy good, though to his own damage; thus must we be content to bear oanothers burden and so fullfill the Law of Christ.

That distinction which is put between the Lawes of God and the lawes of men, becomes a snare to many as it is mis-applied in the ordering of their obedience to civil Authoritie; for when the Authoritie is of God and that in way of an Ordinance Rom. 13. 1. and when the administration of it is according to deductions, and rules gathered from the word of God, and the clear light of nature in civil nations, surely there is no humane law that tendeth to commō good (according to those principles) but the same is mediately a law of God, and that in way of an Ordinance which all are to submit unto and that for conscience sake. Rom. 13. 5.

By order of the Generall Court.

INCREASE NOWEL
SECR.

## THE
## BOOK OF THE GENERAL LAUUES AND
## LIBERTYES CONCERNING &c:

FORASMUCH *as the free fruition of such Liberties, Immunities, priviledges as hu-manitie, civilitie & christianity call for as due to every man in his place, & proportion, without impeachmēt & infringement hath ever been, & ever will be the tranquillity & stability of Churches & Comon-wealths; & the deniall or deprivall therof the disturbance, if not ruine of both:*

Jt is therfore ordered by this Court, & Authority therof, That no mans life shall be taken away; no mans honour or good name shall be stayned; no mans person shal be arrested, restrained, bannished, dismembred nor any wayes punished; no man shall be deprived of his wife or children; no mans goods or estate shall be taken away from him; nor any wayes indamaged under colour of Law or countenance of Authoritie unles it be by the vertue or equity of some expresse law of the Country warranting the same established by a General Court & sufficiently published; or in case of the defect of a law in any particular case by the word of God. And in capital cases, or in cases concerning dismēbring or banishmēt according to that word to be judged by the General Court [1641

### Abilitie.

All persons of the age of twenty one years, and of right understanding & memorie whether excōmunicate, condemned or other, shall have full power and libertie to make their Wills & Testaments & other lawfull Alienations of their lands and estates. [1641]
*see children.*

*see children.*

### Actions.

All Actions of debt, accounts, slaunder, and Actions of the case concerning debts and accounts shal henceforth be tryed where the Plantiffe pleaseth; so it be in the jurisdiction of that Court where the Plantiffe, or Defendant dwelleth: unles by consent under both their hands it appeare they would have the case tryed in any other Court. All other Actions shal be tryed within that jurisdiction where the cause of the Action doth arise. [1642]

2 Jt is ordered by this Court & Authoritie therof, That every person impleading another in any court of Assistants, or County court shal pay the sum of ten shillings before his case be entred, vnles the court see cause to admit any to sue in *forma pauperis.* [1642]

3 Jt is ordered by the Authority aforesayd, That where the debt or damage recovered shall amount to ten pounds in every such case to pay five shillings more, and where it shall amount to twenty pounds or upward there to pay ten shillings more then the first ten shillings, which sayd additions shall be put to the Iudgement and Execution to be levied by the Marshall and accounted for to the Treasurer. [1647]

4 In all actions brought to any court the Plantiffe shall have liberty to withdraw his action or to be non-suted before the Jurie have given in their verdict; in which case he shall alwayes pay full cost and charges to the Defendant, and may afterward renew his sute at another Court. [1641] *see Causes. see Records.*

### Age.

Jt is ordered by this Court & the Authoritie therof, that the age for passing away of lands, or such kinde of hered taments, or for giving of votes, verdicts or sentences in any civil courts or causes, shall be twenty and one years: but in case of chusing of Guardions, fourteen years. [1641 1647]

### Ana-Baptists.

*Forasmuch as experience hath plentifully & often proved that since the first arising of the Ana-baptists about a hundred years past they have been the Incendiaries of Common-wealths & the Infectors of persons in main matters of Religiō, & the Troublers of Churches in most places where they have been, & that they who have held the baptizing of Infants ūlawful, have usually held other errors or heresies together therwith (though as hereticks use to doe they have concealed the same untill they espied a fit advantage and opportunity to vent them by way of question or scruple) and wheras divers of*

*Margin notes:*

Excōmūicate & condemned persons may dispose of their estates

where all act & shal be tryed.

Fees 10 ſs.

more 5 ſs.
more 10 ſs.

Libertie to withdraw or be nonsuted.

Full age and Age of discretion.

A 3                                                                        this

this kinde have since our comming into New-England appeared amongst our selvs, some wherof as others before them have armed the Ordinance of Magistracy, and the lawfulnes of making warre, others the lawfulnes of Magistrats, and their Inspection into any breach of the first Table: which opinions if conived at by us are like to be increased among us & so necessarily bring guilt upō us, infection, & trouble to the Churches & hazzard to the whole Common-wealth:

*Oppose Bapt: &c.*

It is therfore ordered by this Court & Authoritie therof, that if any person or persons within this Iurisdiction shall either openly condemn or oppose the baptizing of Infants, or goe about secretly to seduce others from the approbation or use therof, or shal purposely depart the Congregation at the administration of that Ordinance, or shal deny the Ordinance of Magistracy, or their lawfull right or authoritie to make warr, or to punish the outward breaches of the first Table, and shall appear to the Court willfully

*continue obstinate. Banished.*

and obstinately to continue therin, after due meanes of conviction, every such person or persons shall be sentenced to Banishment. [1644]

## Appeale.

It is ordered by this Court and the Authoritie therof, that it shall be in the libertie of every man cast, condemned, or sentenced in any Inferiour Court, to make his appeal

*Appeal to shire Courts.*

to the Court of Assistants. As also to appeal from the sentence of one Magistrate and other persons deputed to hear and determine small causes, unto the shire Courts of each Iurisdiction where the cause was determined. Provided they tender their appeal and

*Securitie to prosecute &c. Execution respited. Criminal causes*

put in securitie before the Iudges of the Court or other persons authorized to admit Appeals to prosecute it to effect; and also to satisfie all damages before execution granted, which shal not be till twelve hours after judgement, except by special order of the court: and if the cause be of a criminal and not capital nature [in which case wee admit no appeal unles where two of five or three of six or seven, or such a proportion of the number of Magistrats or other Iudges then present shall actually dissent] then also to put in securitie for the good behaviour and appearance at the same time. And if the point of ap-

*Matter of { [Law [Fact*

peal be in matter of law then to be determined by the Bench: if in matter of fact, by the Bench and Iurie. And it is further ordered that all appeales with the securitie as aforesayd shall be recorded at the charge of the partie appealing and certified unto the Court to which they are made.

2 Wheras the Countrye is put to great charges by this Court's attending sutes commenced or renewed either by appeal, petition or review: It is ordered by this Court & Authoritie therof, That in all such cases if it appear to the Court that the Plantiffe in any such action, appeal, petition or review hath no just cause of any such proceeding the said Plantiffe shall bear the whole charges of the Court both for time and expences which they shall judge to have been expended by his occasion: and may further impose a fine upon him as the merit of the cause shall require, but if they shal finde the Defendant in fault they shall impose the charges upon such Defendant. [1642] [1647] *see Causes. see High-wayes. see Lying. see Townships;*

## Appearance Non-apearance.

It is ordered by this Court and Authoritie therof, That no man shall be punished for not appearing at or before any civil Assemblie, Court, Council, Magistrate or Officer; nor for the omission of any Office or service if he shall be necessarily hindred by any apparent act or providence of God which he could neither foresee nor avoid: provided that this law shall not prejudice any person of his just cost and damage in any civil Actiō. [1641] *see Armes. see Indians. see Militry. see Summons.*

## Arrests.

It is ordered and decreed by this Court & Authoritie therof, That no mans person

*None arrested or imprisoned.*

shall be arrested or imprisoned for any debt or fine if the law can finde any competent meanes of satisfaction otherwise from his estate. And if not his person may be arrested and imprisoned, where he shall be kept at his own charge, not the Plantffs, till satisfaction be made; unles the Court that had cognisance of the cause or some s per our Court shall otherwise determine: provided neverthelesse that no mans person shall be kept in prison for debt but when there appears some estate which he will not

produce

produce, to which end any Court or Commissioners authorized by the General Court may administer an oath to the partie or any others suspected to be privie in concealing his estate, but shall satisfie by service if the Creditor require it but shall not be solde to any but of the English nation. [1641: 1647] *see sect 1. page 1.*

## Attachments.

It is ordered by this Court and Authoritie therof that no attachment shall be granted in any civil action to any Forreigner against a setled Inhabitant in this Jurisdiction before he hath given sufficient securitie or caution to prosecute his action and to answer the defendant such costs as the Court shall award him.    And further it is ordered that in all attachments of goods and chattels, or of lands, or hereditaments legall notice shall be given unto the partie or left in writing at his house, or place of usuall aboad, otherwise the sute shall not proceed;  notwithstanding if he be out of this Jurisdiction the cause shall then proceed to triall, but judgement shall not be entered before the next court.    And if the Defendant doe not then appear judgement shall be entered but execution shall not be granted before the Plantife hath given securitie to be responsall to the Defendant if he shall reverse the judgement within one year or such further time as the Court shall limit. [1644] *see actions. see El. writts. see Presidents. see Rates. see Recorder.*

Forreigner shal not attach Inhabitats without cautiõ.

Respit of judgement Of execution.

## Bakers.

It is ordered by this Court and Authoritie therof, that henceforth every Baker shall have a distinct mark for his bread,  & keep the true assizes as heerafter is expressed *viz.* When wheat is ordinarily sold at these severall rates heerafter mentioned the penie white loaf by averdupois weight shall weigh when wheat is by the bushell - - - - - - - at 3 ss. 0 d. The white 11 oũces 1 qr. wheaten 17 oũc. 1 qr. houshould 23 oũc. 0.

| at | | | | | | |
|---|---|---|---|---|---|---|
| at 3 | 6 | 10 | 1 | 15 | 1 | 20 | 2. |
| at 4 | 0 | 09 | 1 | 14 | 0 | 18 | 2. |
| at 4 | 6 | 08 | 1 | 11 | 3 | 16 | 2. |
| at 5 | 0 | 07 | 3 | 11 | 2 | 15 | 2. |
| at 5 | 6 | 07 | 0 | 10 | 2 | 14 | 0. |
| at 6 | 0 | 06 | 2 | 10 | 0 | 13 | 0. |
| at 6 | 6 | 06 | 0 | 09 | 2 | 12 | 2. |

and so proportionably :  under the penaltie of forfeiting all such bread as shall not be of the severall assizes as is aforementioned to the use of the poor of the towne where the offence is committed, and otherwise as is heerafter expressed:    and for the better execution of this present Order ;  there shall be in everie market towne, and all other townes needfull, one or two able persons annually chosen by each towne, who shall be sworn at the next county Court. or by the next Magistrate, unto the faithfull discharge of his or their office; who are heerby authorized to enter into all houses, either with a Constable or without where they shall suspect or be informed of any bread baked for sale: & also to weigh the said bread as oft as they see cause: and to seize all such as they finde defective.    As also to weigh all butter made up for sale; and bringing unto, or being in the towne or market to be solde by weight: which if found light after notice once given shall be forfeited in like manner.    The like penaltie shall be for not marking all bread made for sale.    and the sayd officer shall have one third part of all forfeitures for his paines;  the rest to the poor as aforesayd. [1646]

Penaltie.

Clerk of market. Their power.

Butter.

bread not marked. Clerks fee.

## Ballast.

It is ordered by this Court and Authoritie therof; that no ballast shall be taken frõ any towne shore by any person whatsoever without allowance under the hands of the select men upon the penalty of sixpence for every shovel-full so taken; unles such stones as they had layd there before.    2 It is also ordered by the Authoritie aforesayd; that no ship nor other vessell shall cast out any ballast in the chanel, or other place inconvenient, in any Harbour within this Jurisdiction upon the penaltie of ten pounds. [1646-1642]

Penaltie.

Penaltie.

## Barratrie.

It is ordered, decreed and by this Court declared; that if any man be proved and

and judged a common barrater, vexing others with unjuſt, frequent and endles ſutes: it ſhall be in the power of Courts both to reject his cauſe and to puniſh him for his Barratrie. [1641]

## Benevolence.

Jt is decreed, that this Court heerafter will graunt no benevolence, except in forreigne occaſions & when there is mony in the Treaſurie ſufficient and our debts firſt ſatiſfied. [1641]

## Bills.

Jt is ordered by the Authority of this Court that any debt, or debts due upon bill, or other ſpecialtie aſſigned to another; ſhall be as good a debt & eſtate to the Aſſignee as it was to the Aſſigner at the time of it's aſſignation. And that it ſhall be lawfull for the ſayd Aſſignee to ſue for and recover the ſaid debt, due upon bill, and ſo aſſigned, as fully as the originall creditor might have done, provided the ſaid aſſignement be made upon the backſide of the bill or ſpecialtie. [1647] *ſee uſurie.*

## Bond-ſlavery.

Jt is ordered by this Court and authoritie therof, that there ſhall never be any bond-ſlavery, villenage or captivitie amongſt us; unleſſe it be lawfull captives, taken in juſt warrs, and ſuch ſtrangers as willingly ſell themſelves, or are ſolde to us: and ſuch ſhall have the libertyes and chriſtian uſages which the law of God eſtabliſhed in Iſrael concerning ſuch perſons doth morally require, provided, this exempts none from ſervitude who ſhall be judged thereto by Authoritie. [1641]

## Bounds of townes and perſons.

Foraſmuch as the bounds of townes & of the lands of particular perſons are carefully to be maintained, & not without great danger to be removed by any, which notwithſtanding by deficiency and decay of marks, may at unawars be done, whereby great jealouſies of perſons, trouble in townes and incumbrances in courts do often ariſe, which by due care and meanes might be prevented: — — —

**Boundes of towne ſet out within 12 mon.**

Jt is therefore ordered by this Court and the Authoritie therof, that every towne ſhall ſet out their bounds within twelve months after their bounds are graunted. And that when their bounds are once ſet out: once in the year three or more perſons of a

**Perambulation**

towne, appoynted by the ſelect men, ſhall appoynt with the adjacent townes to go the bounds betwixt their ſaid townes, and renew their marks; which marks ſhal be a great heap of ſtones, or a trench of ſix foot long and two foot broad. The moſt ancient town to give notice of the time and place of meeting for this perambulation. Which time

**Jn 1 or 2 mō. on payn of 5 li**

ſhall be in the firſt or ſecond month, upon payne of five pounds for everie towne that ſhall neglect the ſame; provided that the three men appoynted for perambulation ſhall goe in their ſeverall quarters by order of the Select men and at the charge of the ſeverall townes.

**Particular perambu:**

And it is further ordered that if any particular proprietor of lands lying in common with others ſhall refuſe to goe the bounds betwixt his land and other mens once a yeare in the firſt or ſecond month, being requeſted therunto upon one weeks warning,

**Pænalty 10 ſs.**

he ſhall forfeit for every day ſoe neglecting, ten ſhillings, halfe to the partie moving thereto, the other halfe to the towne. [1641 1647]

## Burglarie and Theft.

Foraſmuch as many perſons of late years have been, and are apt to be injurious to the goods and lives of others, notwithſtanding all care and meanes to prevent and puniſh the ſame; — — —

**Houſe, field or high wayes. Firſt offence.**

. Jt is therefore ordered by this Court and Authoritie therof that if any perſon ſhall commit Burglarie by breaking up any dwelling houſe, or ſhall rob any perſon in the field, or high wayes; ſuch a perſon ſo offending ſhall for the firſt offence be branded on the forehead with the letter ( Ђ ) If he ſhall offend in the ſame kinde the ſecond time, he ſhall be branded as before and alſo be ſeverally whipped: and if he ſhall fall

**Third offence death.**

into the like offence the third time he ſhall be put to death, as being incorrigible. And if any perſon ſhal commit ſuch Burglarie, or rob in the fields or houſe on the Lords day

besides

besides the former punishments, he shal for the first offence have one of his ears cut off. And for the second offence in the same kinde he shal loose his other ear in the same māner. And if he fall into the same offence a third time he shal be put to death if it appear to the Court he did it presumptuously. [1642 1647]

2 For the prevention of Pilfring and Theft, it is ordered by this Court and Authoritie therof; that if any person shal be taken or known to rob any orchard or garden, that shall hurt, or steal away any grafts or fruit trees, fruits, linnen, woollen, or any other goods left out in orchards, gardens, backsides, or any other place in house or fields: or shall steal any wood or other goods from the water-side, from mens doors, or yards; he shall forfeit treble damage to the owners therof. And if they be children, or servants that shall trespasse heerin, if their parents or masters will not pay the penaltie before expressed, they shal be openly whipped. And forasmuch as many times it so falls out that small thefts and other offences of a criminall nature, are committed both by English & Indian, in townes remote from any prison, or other fit place to which such malefactors may be committed till the next Court, it is therfore heerby ordered; that any Magistrate upon complaint made to him may hear, and upon due proof determin any such small offences of the aforesayd nature, according to the laws heer established, and give warrant to the Constable of that town where the offender lives to levie the same: provided the damage or fine exceed not fourty shillings: provided also it shall be lawfull for either partie to appeal to the next Court to be holden in that Jurisdiction, giving sufficient caution to prosecute the same to effect at the said Court. And everie Magistrate shall make return yearly to the Court of that Jurisdiction wherin he liveth of what cases he hath so ended. And also the Constables of all such fines as they have received. And where the offender hath nothing to satisfie such Magistrate may punish by stocks, or whipping as the cause shall deserve, not exceeding ten stripes. It is also ordered that all servants & workmen imbeazling the goods of their masters, or such as set them on work shal make restitution and be lyable to all lawes & penalties as other men. [1646]

## CAPITAL LAWES.

IF any man after legal conviction shall HAVE OR WORSHIP any other God, but the LORD GOD: he shall be put to death. *Exod.* 22.20. *Deut.* 13.6. & 10. *Deut.* 17.2.6.

2 If any man or woman be a WITCH, that is, hath or consulteth with a familiar spirit, they shall be put to death. *Exod.* 22.18. *Levit.* 20.27. *Deut.* 18.10.11.

3 If any person within this Jurisdiction whether Christian or Pagan shall wittingly and willingly presume to BLASPHEME the holy Name of God, Father, Son or Holy-Ghost, with direct, expresse, presumptuous, or high-handed blasphemy, either by wilfull or obstinate denying the true God, or his Creation, or Government of the world: or shall curse God in like manner, or reproach the holy Religion of God as if it were but a politick device to keep ignorant men in awe; or shal utter any other kinde of Blasphemy of the like nature & degree they shall be put to death. *Levit.* 24.15.16.

4 If any person shall commit any wilfull MURTHER, which is Man slaughter, committed upon premeditate malice, hatred, or crueltie not in a mans necessary and just defence, nor by meer casualty against his will, he shall be put to death. *Exod.* 21.12.13. *Numb.* 35.31.

5 If any person slayeth another suddenly in his ANGER, or CRUELTY of passion, he shall be put to death. *Levit.* 24.17. *Numb.* 35.20.21.

6 If any person shall slay another through guile, either by POYSONING, or other such devilish practice, he shall be put to death. *Exod.* 21.14.

7 If any man or woman shall LYE WITH ANY BEAST, or bruit creature, by carnall copulation; they shall surely be put to death: and the beast shall be slain, & buried, and not eaten. *Lev.* 20.15.16.

8 If any man LYETH WITH MAN-KINDE as he lieth with a woman, both of them have committed abomination, they both shal surely be put to death: unles the one partie were forced (or be under fourteen years of age in which case he shall be seveerly punished

B

*Margin notes:*
Lords day.
Rob [orchard. [garden. Steal goods.
Treble damage.
Whipped.
One Magistr: may hear & determine.
Appeal. Magistrate and Cost: to make return
Stocks or whip
Servants and workmen.
Idolatrie.
Witch-craft.
Blasphemie.
Murther.
Poysoning.
Bestialitie.
Sodomie. Genis. 19.5.

punished) *Levit.* 20. 13.

**Adulterie.**

9 If any person commit ADULTERIE with a married, or espoused wife; the Adulterer & Adulteresse shal surely be put to death. *Lev.*20. 19. & 18. 20. *Deu.* 22. 23. 27

**Man-stealing.**

10 If any man STEALETH A MAN, or Man-kinde, he shall surely be put to death *Exodus* 21. 16.

**False-wittnes.**

11 If any man rise up by FALSE-WITNES wittingly, and of purpose to take away any mans life: he shal be put to death. *Deut.* 19. 16. 18. 16.

**Conspiracie.**

12 If any man shall CONSPIRE, and attempt any Invasion, Insurrection, or publick Rebellion against our Common-Wealth: or shall indeavour to surprize any Town, or Townes, Fort, or Forts therin; or shall treacherously, & perfidiously attempt the Alteration and Subversion of our frame of Politie, or Government fundamentally he shall be put to death. *Numb.* 16. 2 *Sam.* 3. 2 *Sam.* 18. 2 *Sam.* 20.

**Child curse or smite parēts**

13 If any child, or children, above sixteen years old, and of sufficient understanding, shall CURSE, or SMITE their natural FATHER, or MOTHER; he or they shall be put to death : unles it can be sufficiently testified that the Parents have been very unchristianly negligent in the education of such children; or so provoked them by extream, and cruel correction; that they have been forced therunto to preserve themselves from death or maiming, *Exod.* 21. 17. *Lev.* 20. 9. *Exod.* 21. 15.

**Rebellious Sō**

14 If a man have a stubborn or REBELLIOUS SON, of sufficient years & ūderstanding ( *viz* ) sixteen years of age, which will not obey the voice of his Father, or the voice of his Mother, and that when they have chastened him will not harken unto them: then shal his Father & Mother being his natural parēts, lay hold on him, & bring him to the Magistrates assembled in Court & testifie unto them, that their Son is stubborn & rebellious & will not obey their voice and chastisement, but lives in sundry notorious crimes, such a son shal be put to death. *Deut.* 21. 20. 21.

**Rape.**

15 If any man shal RAVISH any maid or single womā, cōmitting carnal copulation with her by force, against her own will; that is above the age of ten years he shal be punished either with death, or with some other grievous punishment according to circumstances as the Judges, or General court shal determin. [1641]

### Cask & Cooper.

**London assize.**

**Gager**

**his Fee.**

**Who shall appoint Gager.**

**Coopers brand**

It is ordered by this Court and authoritie therof, that all cask used for any liquor, fish, or other cōmoditie to be put to sale shall be of London assize, and that fit persons shal be appointed from time to time in all places needfull, to gage all such vessels or cask & such as shal be found of due assize shal be marked with the Gagers mark, & no other who shal have for his paines four pence for every tun, & so proportionably. And every County court or any one Magistrate upon notice given them shall appoint such Gagers to view the said cask, & to see that they be right, & of sound & wel seasoned timber, & that everie Cooper have a distinct brand-mark on his own cask, upon payn of forfeiture of twenty shilling in either case, & so proportiōably for lesser vessels. [1642 1647]

### Cattel. Corn-fields. Fences.

**each party make good his fence.**
**No catle put in till corn be out**

It is ordered by this Court and authoritie therof, That in all corn-fields, which are inclosed in common: everie partie interested therin, shall from time to time make good his part of the fence, and shall not put in any cattel, so long as any corn shal be upon any part of it, upon payn to answer all the damage which shal come therby. [1647]

**Occupiers of land may order cōmon fields**

2 *Wheras it is foūd by experience that there hath been much trouble & difference in severall townes, about the fencing, planting, sowing, seeding & ordering of common fields,* It is therfore ordered by this Court & authoritie therof, that where the occupiers of the land, or of the greatest part therof cānot agree about the fencing or improymēt of such their said fields, that thē the Select men in the several towns shal order the same, or in case where no such are, then the major part of the Freemen (with what convenient speed they may) shal determin any such difference, as may arise upon any informatiō given them by the said occupiers, excepting such occupier's land as shal be sufficiently fenced in by it selfe, which any occupier of land may lawfully doe. [1643. 1647]

**Exe: pertic: fenced.**

3 *Wheras this Court hath long since provided that all men shall fence their corn, meadow*

*ground*

ground and such like against great cattle, to the end the increase of cattle especially of cowes and their breed should not be hindred, there being then but few horses in the countrie, which since are much increased, many wherof run in a sort wilde, doing much damage in corn and other things, notwithstanding fences made up according to the true intent of the order in that case established: many wherof are unknown, most so unruly that they can by no means be caught, or got into custodie, wherby their owners might answer damages: & if sometimes with much difficultie and charge they be; they are in danger of perishing before the owner appears or can be found out: all which to prevent,

It is ordered by this Court & authoritie therof; That everie towne and peculiar in this Jurisdictiõ, shall henceforth give some distinct Brand-mark appointed by this court (a coppie of which marks each Clerk of writs in everie town shal keep a record of) upon the horn, or left buttock or shoulder of all their cattle which feed in open cõmon without constant keepers, wherby it may be known to what town they doe belong. And if any trespasse not so marked they shall pay double damages: nor shall any person knowing, or after due notice given of any beast of his to be unruly in respect of fences, suffer him or them to go in cõmon or against corn fields, or other impropriate inclosed grouds fenced as aforesaid, without such shackles or fetters as may restrein and prevent trespasse therin by them from time to time. And if any horse or other beast trespasse in corn, or other inclosure being fenced in such sort as secures against cows, oxen and such like orderly cattel: the partie or parties trespassed shall procure two sufficient Inhabitants of that town, of good repute and credit to view and adjudge the harms, which the owner of the beast shal satisfie, when known, upõ reasonable demand, whether the beast were impounded or not. But if the owner be known, or neer residing as in the same town or the like, he shall forthwith have notice of the trespasse and damage charged upon him, that if he approve not therof he may nominate one such man, who with one such other chosen by the partie damnified as aforesaid, shal review & adjudge the said harms, provided they agree of damage within one day after due notice given, & that no after harms intervene to hinder it. Which being forthwith discharged, together with the charge of the notice, former view and determination of damages, the first judgement shall be void, or else to stand good in law. And if any cattle be found damage faisant, the partie damnified may impound or keep them in his own private close, or yard till he may give notice to the owner, and if they cannot agree, the owner may replevie them, or the other partie may retur them to the owner & take his remedie according to law. [1647]

4 It is ordered by the authoritie of this Court that for all harms done by goats, there shall be double damages allowed: and that any goats taken in corn or gardens, the owners of such corn or gardens may keep or use the said goats till full satisfaction be made by the owners of such goats. [1646]

5 Forasmuch as complaints have been made of a verie evil practice, of some disordered persons in the countrie, who use to take other mens horses, somtimes upon the commons and somtimes out of their own grounds, and inclosures, and ride them at their pleasure without any leave or privitie of the owners:

It is therfore ordered and enacted by the authoritie of this Court, that whosoever shall take any other mans horse, mare, asse or drawing beast, either out of his inclosure, or upon any common or elsewhere, (except such be taken damage faisant and disposed of according to law) without leave of the owner: & shall ride or use the same, he shal pay to the partie wronged, treble damages, or if the complainant shall desire it then to pay only ten shillings, and such as have not to make satisfaction, shall be punished by whipping, imprisonment, or otherwise as by law shal be adjudged, and any one Magistrate or County court may hear & determin the same. [1647]

6 For the better preserving of corn from damage by all kinde of cattle, and that all fences of corn fields may from time to time be sufficiently upheld and maintained;

It is therfore ordered that the Select men of every town within this Jurisdiction shall appoynt from year to year two (or more if need require) of the Inhabitants therof to view the cõmon fences of everie their corn fields, to the end, to take due notice of the
reall

     B 2

*Marginal notes:*
Double damage.
Fetters,
Harms viewed
Notice of damage.
Damage faisant
Goats shall pay double damage
Unruly taken
Penaltie.
Corporal punishment
One Magistr: power:
Select men to appoint men to view fence:

reall defects and insufficiencie therof, who shall forthwith acquaint the owners therof
with the same: and if the said owners do not within six dayes time or otherwise as the
Select men shall appoint, sufficiently repair their said defective fences, then the said two
or more Inhabitants appointed as aforesayd shall forthwith repair or renew them and
shall have double recompence, for all their labour, care, cost and trouble, to be payd by
the owners of the said insufficient fence or fences, and shall have warrant from the sayd

Select men directed to the Constable to levie the same, either upon the corn or other e-
state of the delinquent. Provided the defect of the fence or fences be sufficiently proved
by two or three wittnesses. [1647]

7 Where lands lye in common unfenced, if one man shall improve his lands by fencing in severall & another shall not, he who shall so improve shall secure his land agairst
other mens cattle; & shall not compel such as joyne upon him to make any fence with
him; except he shall also improve in severall as the other doth. And where one man
shal improve before his neighbour & so make the whole fence, if after his said neighbour
shall improve also, he shal then satisfie for halfe the others fence against him, according
to the present value and shall maintain the same: and if the first man shall after lay open
his said field, then the sayd neighbour shal injoye his said halfe fence so purchased to his
own use, & shal also have libertie to buy the other halfe fence paying according to present valuation to be set by two men chosen by either partie one: the like order shal be
where any man shall improve land against any town cõmon. provided this order shall

not extend to house lots not exceeding ten acres, but if in such, one shall improve, his
neighbour shal be compellable to make & maintain one half of the fence between them

whether he improve or not. Provided also that no man shall be lyable to satisfie for damage done in any ground not sufficiently fenced except it shall be for damage done by
swine or calves under a year old, or unruly cattle which will not be restreined by ordinary fences, or where any man shall put his cattle, or otherwise voluntarily trespasse upon
his neighbours ground, & if the partie damnified finde the cattle damage faisant he may
impound or otherwise dispose of them as in Sect: 3. [1642]

### Causes. Small causes.

For easing the charge & incumbrance of courts by small causes, It is ordered by
this Court and authoritie therof, That any Magistrate in the town where he dwells may
hear and determin by his discretion (not by Jurie) according to the laws heer established,

all causes arising in that County wherin the debt, trespasse or damage doth not exceed
fourty shillings, who may send for parties, & wittnesses by Sũmons or Attachment directed to the Constable who shall faithfully execute the same. And it is further ordered

that in such towns where no Magistrate dwells, the Court of Assistants or County court
for each Shire shall from time to time upon request of the said towns signified under the
hands of the Constable appoint three of the Freemen as Commissioners in such cases any
two wherof shall have like power to hear and determin by their discretion (not by Jurie)

all such causes aforesaid according to the laws heer establ.shed, who also have heerby
power to send for part es and wittnesses by Sũmons or Attachment directed to the Constable, as also to administer oaths to wittnesses & to give time to the Defendãt to answer

if they see cause, & if the partie sentenced refuse to give his own bond for appearance or
satisfaction where no goods appear in the same town where the Plantiffe or Defendant
dwells, they may charge the Constable with the partie to carry him before a Magistrate
or Shire court (if then sitting) to be further proceeded with according to law; but the

said three men may not commit to prison in any case. And it is further ordered that such
as be found in any town shall be lyable to be sued in that town at libertie of the Plantiff.

*And forasmuch as the Governour, Deputy Governour and Assistants are under an oath of
God for dispencing equal justice according to law,* It is ordered by the Authoritie afore-

said; that henceforth all Associates for County courts when and where there be any; and
all such Freemẽ authorized as aforesayd, shall be sworn before each Shire court, or some
Magistrate in that County unto the faithfull discharge of the trust and power committed
to them

to them. And it is further ordered by the Authoritie aforesaid, that in all small causes as aforesayd, where only one Magistrate dwells within the town, and the cause concerns himselfe, as also in such towns where no Magistrate is, and the cause concerns any of the three Freemen aforementioned, that in such cases the five, seven, or other number of Selected townsmen shall have power to hear and determin the same: and also to graunt execution for the levying, and gathering up such damages, for the use of the person damnified. And any Court may reject any such cause in all the cases beforementioned in this law, if it were not first brought to the power heerby authorized in towns to end the same. [1647]

*Charges publick.*

Is is ordered by this Court that no Governour, Deputy Gover: Assistant, Associate, Grand, or Petty Jurie-man, at any court; nor any Deputie for the General court, nor any Comissioner for martial disciplin at the time of their publick meetings; shall at any time bear his own charges: but their necessary expences shal be defrayed either by the town, or the Shire on whose service they are, or by the Country in generall. [1634. 1641]

2 It is ordered by this Court that in all ordinary publick works of the Comon-weal, one Assistant and the Overseer of the work shal have power to send their warrants to the Constables of the next towns to send so many labourers & artificers as the warrant shall direct, which the Constable and two other or more of the Freemen which he shall take to himselfe shall forthwith execute: for which service such Assistant and Overseer aforsaid shall have power to give such extraordinary wages as they shall judge the work to deserve. Provided that for any ordinary work no man shal be compelled to work from home above a week together. And for all extraordinarie publick works it is ordered that one Assistant & the Overseer of the said work shall have power to send their warrants to the Constable of any town for so many men of any condicō except Magistrates & Officers of Churches and Comon-wealth, as the warrant shal direct, which the Constable & two or more that he shal chuse shal forthwith send: to advise & attēd the same. 1634

3 *This Court taking into consideration the necessity of an equal contribution to all common charges in towns, and observing that the cheif occasion of the defect heerin ariseth from hence, that many of those who are not Freemen, nor members of any Church doe take advantage therby to withdraw their help in such voluntary contributions as are in use.*

It is therfore ordered by this Court and Authoritie therof, That everie Inhabitant shal henceforth contribute to all charges both in Church & Commonwealth wherof he doth or may receive benefit: and every such Inhabitant who shal not voluntarily contribute proportionably to his ability with the Freemen of the same town to all comon charges both civil and ecclesiastical shall be compelled thereto by assessment & distresse to be levied by the Constable or other Officer of the town as in other cases: and that the lands & estates of all men (wherever they dwell) shall be rated for all town charges both civil and ecclesiasticall as aforesaid where the lands and estates shal lye: their persons where they dwell. [1638 1643 1644]

4 *For a more equall and ready way of raysing meanes for defraying publick charges in time to come: and for preventing such inconveniences as have fallen out upon former assessments; It is ordered and enacted by the authoritie of this Court,* That the Treasurer for the time being shal from year to year in the first month without expecting any other order send forth his warrants to the Constables & Select men of every town within this Jurisdiction, requiring the Constable to call together the Inhabitants of the town who being so assembled: shal chuse some one of their Freemen to be a Commissioner for the town, who together with the Select men for their prudential affairs shall some time or times in the sixt month then next ensuing make a List of all the male persons in the same town, from sixteen years old & upwards; and a true estimation of all personall & real estates, being, or reputed to be the estate of all & everie the persons in the same town, or otherwise under their custody, or managing according to just valuation, and to what persons the same doe belong whether in their own town or other where, so neer as they can by all lawful wayes and means which they may use. viz: of houses, lands

B 3          of all

Can: concer: Magistr: & Comissi:

Sel: men may end.

court reject such cause if not first heard as aforsd:

Magi: & offic: charges

how defrayed

Publ: works:

sutable wages

persons exem:

Every Inhabit: pay to Ch. & comon-weal.

or distreined

Land & estate to pay where they are.

Rates. Tres: to send war: to towns every 6 mon:

of all forts as well unbroken up as other (except fuch as doth or fhal lye common for free feed of cattle to the ufe of the inhabitants in generall whether belonging to towns, or particular perfons but not to be kept or hearded upõ it to the damage of the Proprietors) mills, fhips & all fmall veffells, merchantable goods, cranes, wharfes & all forts of cattle & all other known eftate whatfoever; as alfo all vifible eftate either at fea or on fhore all which perfons and eftates are by the faid Commiffioners & Select men to be affeffed, and rated as heer followeth *viz*: every perfon aforefaid except Magiftrates and Elders of Churches, two fhillings fixpence by the head, & all eftates both reall & perfonall at one pennie for everie twenty fhillings, according to the rates of cattle heerafter mentioned. And for a more certein rule in rating of cattle: everie cow of four year olde and upward fhall be valued at five pounds, everie heifer, and fteer betwixt three and four years old four pounds, and between two & three years old at fifty fhillings, and between one and two years thirty fhillings: everie ox & bull of four year old & upward fix pounds. Everie horfe & mare of four year old and upward feven pounds, of three year old five poũds between two and three year old three pounds, of one year old fourtie fhillings. Everie fheep above one year old thirty fhillings: everie goat above one year old eight fhillings: everie fwine above one year old twenty fhillings: everie affe above one year old fourty fhillings. And all cattel of all forts under a year old are heerby exempted, as alfo all hay and corn in the husbandmans hand, becaufe all meadow, arrable ground and cattle are ratable as aforefaid. And for all fuch perfons as by the advantage of their arts & trades are more enabled to help bear the publick charge then common laborours and workmẽ, as Butchers, Bakers, Brewers, Victuailers, Smiths, Carpenters, Taylors, fhoe-makers, Joyners, Barbers, Millers & Mafons with all other manuall perfons & artifts, fuch are to be rated for their returns & gains proportionable unto other men for the produce of their eftates. Provided that in the rate by the poll, fuch perfons as are difabled by ficknes, lamenes or other infirmitie fhall be exempted. And for fuch fervants & children as take not wages, their parents and mafters fhall pay for them, but fuch as take wages fhal pay for themfelves. And it is further ordered that the Cõmiffioners for the feverall towns in everie Shire fhall yearly upon the firft fourth day of the week in the feventh month, affemble at their fhire Town: & bring with them fairly written the juft number of males lifted as aforefaid, and the affeffments of eftates made in their feveral towns according to the rules & directions in this prefent order expreffed, and the faid Cõmiffioners being fo affembled fhall duly and carefully examin all the faid lifts and affeffments of the feverall towns in that Shire, and fhall correct & perfect the fame according to the true intent of this order, as they or the major part of them fhal determĩ, & the fame fo perfected they fhal fpeedily tranfmit to the Treafurer ũder their hands or the hands of the major part of them and therupon the Treafurer fhal give warrants to the Conftables to collect & levie the fame; fo as the whole affeffment both for perfons & eftates may be payd in unto the Treafurer before the twentith day of the ninth mõth, yearly, & everie one fhal pay their rate to the Conftable in the fame town where it fhal be affeffed. Nor fhall any land or eftate be rated in any other town but where the fame fhal lye, is, or was improved to the owners, reputed owners or other propietors ufe or behoof if it be within this Jurifdictiõ. And if the Treafurer cañot difpofe of it there, the Conftable fhal fend it to fuch place in *Bofton* or elfwhere as the Treafurer fhall appoint at the charge of the Countrie to be allowed the Conftable upon his accoũt with the Treafurer. And for all peculiars *viz*: fuch places as are not yet layd within the bounds of any town the fame lands with the perfons and eftates therupon fhall be affeffed by the rates of the town next unto it, the meafure or eftimation fhall be by the diftance of the Meeting houfes.

And if any of the faid Commiffioners or of the Select men fhall wittingly fail or neglect to perform the truft committed to them by this Order in not making, correcting, perfecting or tranfmitting any of the faid Lifts or Affeffments according to the intent of this Order; everie fuch offendor fhall be fined fourty fhillings for everie fuch offence, or fo much as the Country fhall be damnified therby, fo as it exceed not fourty fhillings for one offence. Provided that fuch offence or offences be
complained

---

Marginal notes (left column):

All known & vifible eftate

Perfons exempt: frõ pol mony 1 *d.* in the *li.* upon eftate.

Rates of cattle

Artificers &c

Impotent perfons exempt: frõ pol mony

Cõmiffi: meet in 7 month at Shire town

to perfect affeffments,

Conftable to collect & pay in 9 mõth.

Land rated where it lyes

Peculiars

Commiffi: or Select men defaulting

fined 40 *fs.*

complained of and profecuted in due courfe of law within fix months. And it is farther ordered that upon all diftreffes to be taken for any of the rates and affeffments aforefaid: the Officer fhall diftrein goods, or cattle if they may be had, and if no goods then lands or houfes, if neither goods nor lands can be had within the town where fuch diftreffe is to be taken, then upon fuch return to the Treafurer he fhall give warrant to attach the body of fuch perfon to be carried to prifon, there to be kept till the next court of that Shire; except they put in fecuritie for their appearance there, or that payment be made in the mean time . And it is farther ordered that the prizes of all forts of corn to be received upon any rate, by vertue of this order, fhall be fuch as this Court fhall fet from year to year; and in default therof they fhall be accepted at the prcie current to be judged by the fayd Commiffioners of Effex, Midlefex and Suffolk. And it is farther ordered that all eftates of land in England fhall not be rated in any publick affeffment. And it is heerby declared that by publick rates and affeffments , is intended only fuch as are affeffed by order of the General court for the contrys occafion & no other.·[1646 1647]

### Children.

*Forafmuch as the good education of children is of fingular behoof and benefit to any Common-wealth; and wheras many parents & mafters are too indulgent and negligent of their duty in that kinde.* It is therfore ordered that the Select men of everie town, in the feverall precincts and quarters where they dwell, fhall have a vigilant eye over their brethren & neighbours, to fee, firft that none of them fhall fuffer fo much barbarifm in any of their families as not to indeavour to teach by themfelves or others, their children & apprentices fo much learning as may inable them perfectly to read the englifh tongue, & knowledge of the Capital lawes: upõ penaltie of twentie fhillings for each neglect therin. Alfo that all mafters of families doe once a week (at the leaft) catechize their children and fervants in the grounds & principles of Religion, & if any be unable to doe fo much: that then at the leaft they procure fuch children or apprentices to learn fome fhort orthodox catechifm without book, that they may be able to anfwer unto the queftions that fhall be propounded to them out of fuch catechifm by their parents or mafters, or any of the Select men when they fhall call them to a tryall of what they have learned in this kinde. And further that all parents and mafters do breed & bring up their children & apprentices in fome honeft lawful calling, labour or imploymẽt, either in husbandry, or fome other trade profitable for themfelves, and the Common-wealth if they will not or cannot train them up in learning to fit them for higher imployments. And if any of the Select men after admonitiõ by them given to fuch mafters of families fhal finde them ftill negligent of their dutie in the particulars aforementioned, wherby children and fervants become rude, ftubborn & unruly; the faid Select men with the help of two Magiftrates, or the next County court for that Shire, fhall take fuch children or apprentices from them & place them with fome mafters for years (boyes till they come to twenty one, and girls eighteen years of age compleat) which will more ftrictly look unto, and force them to fubmit unto government according to the rules of this order, if by fair means and former inftructions they will not be drawn unto it. [1642]

*2 Wheras fundry Gentlemen of qualitie, and others oft times fend over their children into th's country unto fome freinds heer, hoping at the leaft therby to prevent their extravagant and riotous courfes, who notwithftanding by means of fome unadvifed and ill-affected perfons, which give them credit, in expectation their freinds, either in favour to them, or prevention of blemifh to themfelves, will difcharge what ever is done that way, they are no leffe lavifh & profufe heer to the great greif of their freinds, difhonour of God & reproach of the Countrie.*

It is therfore ordered by this Court & authoritie therof; That if any perfon after publication heerof fhall any way give credit to any fuch youth, or other perfon under twentie one years of age, without order from fuch their freinds, heer, or elfwhere, under their hands in writing they fhall lofe their debt whatever it be . And further if fuch youth or other perfon incur any penalty by fuch means and have not wherwith to pay, fuch perfon, or perfons, as are occafions therof fhall pay it as delinquents in the like cafe fhould doe. [1647] *See Abilitie.*

3 If any

if profecuted fix mon. Conft: direct:

Prizes of corn

Lands in England exempt: Intent of publick rates.

Care of Select men

§ all children may read on pen: of 20 s.

Catechifm

Unruly children

placed forth

Extravagancy

Debts of perfons in nõ-ge not recov.

occafiõers of their difor: to pay their fine.

**Parents denying marriage**

3 If any parents shall wilfully, and unreasonably deny any childe timely or convenient marriage, or shall exercise any unnaturall severitie towards them, such children shal have libertie to complain to Authoritie for redresse in such cases. [1641]

**Orphan not disposed of but by consent of Authority.**

**Minority of women.**

4 No Orphan during their minority which was not committed to tuition, or service by their parents in their life time, shall afterward be absolutely disposed of by any without the consent of some Court wherin two Assistants (at least) shall be present, except in case of marriage, in which the approbation of the major part of the Select men, in that town or any one of the next Assistants shall be sufficient. And the minoritie of women in case of marriage shall be till sixteen years. [1646] *See Age. Cap: Laws. Lib: cōmō: marriage.*

### Clerk of writs.

It is ordered by this Court and Authoritie therof ; that in everie town throughout this Jurisdiction there shall henceforth be a Clerk of the writs nominated by each town and allowed by each shire Court, or court of Assistants to graunt Summons and Attachments in all civil actions : and attachments (or Summons at the libertie of the Plantiffe) shall be graunted when the partie is a stranger not dwelling amongst us or for some that are going out of our Jurisdiction, or that are about to make away their estates to defraud

**Doubtful in estate.**

their creditors , or when persons are doubtfull in their estates not only to the Plantiffe, but to the Clerk of the writs, signified ūder the hands of two honest persons, neer dwelling unto the sayd partie.

**Cl: grant repl:**

Aud the sayd Clerks of writs are authorized to graunt replevins and to take bond with sufficient securitie of the partie to prosecute the Sute whose fees shall be for every Warrant two pence, a Replevin or Attachment three pêce, & for Bonds four pence a peece. All Attachments to be directed unto the Constables in towns where no Marshall is. Also the sayd Clerks shal graunt Sūmons for Witnesses. [1641] *See Recorder.*

### Colledge.

Wheras through the good hand of Goa upon us there is a Colledge founded in Cambridge in the County of Middlsex called Harvard Colledge. for incouragement wherof this Court hath given the summe of four hundred pounds and also the revenue of the Ferrie betwixt Charlstown and Boston and that the well ordering and manueging of the said Colledge is of great concernment,

**Harvard Coll.**

**Cōmissioners.**

It is therfore ordered by this Court and Authoritie therof, That the Governour & Deputie Gover: for the time being and all the Magistrates of this Jurisdiction together with the teaching Elders of the six next adjoyning towns *viz:* Cambridge, Water-town Charlstown, Boston, Roxburie and Dorchester, & the President of the said Colledge for the time being, shal from time to time have full power & authoritie to make and establish

**to establish orders.**

all such orders, statutes and constitutions, as they shall see necessary for the instituting, guiding and furthering of the said Colledge, and several members therof, from time to time, in Pietie, Moralitie & Learning; as also to dispose, order and manage to the use

**dispose gifts & reven.**

and behoof of the said Colledge and members therof, all gifts, legacyes, bequeaths, revenues, lands and donations as either have been, are, or shall be conferred, bestowed, or any wayes shall fall or come to the sayd Colledge. And wheras it may come to passe that many of the Magistrates and said Elders may be absent and otherwise imployed in other weighty affairs whē the said Colledge may need their present help and counsell.

**power of major part.**

It is therfore ordered that the greater number of Magistrates and Elders which shall be present with the President, shall have the power of the whole. Provided that if any constitution, order or orders by them made shall be found hurtfull unto the said Colledg, or the members therof, or to the weal publick then upō appeal of the partie or parties greived, unto the company of Overseers first mentioned, they shal repeal the said order or orders (if they see cause) at their next meeting or stand accountable therof to the next Generall court. [1636 1640 1642]

**Lib: of appeal**

**Power to rep.**

### Condemned.

**None exec: within 4 days**

It is ordered by this Court that no man condemned to dye shall be put to death within four dayes next after his condemnation, unles the Court see speciall cause to the
contrary

contrary, or in caſe of martial-law: nor ſhall the body of any man ſo put to death be unburied twelve hours unleſs it be in caſe of anatomy. [1641]

### Conſtables.

It is ordered by this Court, That Conſtables are to whip or puniſh any to be puniſhed by order of Authoritie (where there is not another officer appointed to doe it) in their own towns; unleſs they can get another to do it.

2 It is farther ordered by the Authoritie aforeſaid, That any perſon tendered to any Conſtable of this Juriſdiction by any Conſtable or other Officer belonging to any forreign Juriſdiction in this Countrie, or by warrant from any ſuch authoritie, ſuch ſhall preſently be received, and conveyed forthwith from Conſtable to Conſtable, till they be brought unto the place to which they are ſent, or before ſome Magiſtrate of this Juriſdiction who ſhall diſpoſe of them as the juſtice of the cauſe ſhall require. And that all Hue-&-cries ſhall be duly received and dilligently purſued to full effect. [1641][1642]

3 It is ordered by the authoritie of this Court, That everie Conſtable within our juriſdiction ſhall henceforth have full power to make, ſigne & put forth Purſutes or Hue-&-cries after Murtherers, Manſlayers, Peace-breakers, Theevs, Robbers, Burglarers and other Capital offenders, where no Magiſtrate is neer hand, alſo to apprehend without Warrant, ſuch as are overtaken with drink, ſwearing, Sabboth-breaking, lying, vagrant perſons, night-walkers, or any other that ſhall offend in any of theſe. Provided they be taken in the manner, either by ſight of the Conſtable, or by preſent informatiō from others. As alſo to make ſearch for all ſuch perſons, either on the Sabboth day or other, when there ſhal be occaſion, in all houſes licenſed to ſell either beer or wine, or in any other ſuſpected or diſordered places, and thoſe to apprehend and keep in ſafe cuſtodie, till opportunitie ſerve to bring them before one of the next Magiſtrates for farther examination. Provided when any Conſtable is imployed by any of the Magiſtrates for apprehending of any perſon, he ſhall not doe it without warrant in writing, and if any perſon ſhall refuſe to aſſiſt any Conſtable in the executiō of his office, in any of the things aforementiōed being by him required therto, they ſhal pay for neglect therof ten ſhillings, to the uſe of the Country to be levied by warrant from any Magiſtrate before whom any ſuch offender ſhal be brought. And if it appear by good teſtimonie, that any ſhal wilfully, obſtinately or contemptuouſly refuſe or neglect to aſſiſt any Conſtable as is before expreſſed, he ſhall pay to the uſe of the Country fourty ſhillings. And that no man may plead ignorance for ſuch neglect or refuſal, it is ordered that everie Conſtable ſhall have a black ſtaffe of five foot long, tipped at the upper end, about five inches with braſſe, as a badge of his office, which he ſhal take with him when he goeth to diſcharge any part of his office: which ſtaffe ſhall be provided at the charge of the town, and if any Magiſtrate or Conſtable or any other, upon urgent occaſion, ſhall refuſe to doe their beſt indeavours, in raiſing & proſecuting Hue-&-cries by foot, & if need be, by horſe, after ſuch as have cōmitted Capital crimes, they ſhall forfeit for everie ſuch offence to the uſe aforeſaid fourty ſhillings. [1646] See In-keepers, Maſters, Oaths, Rates, Untimely death, watching.

### Conveyances fraudulent.

It is ordered by this Court and the Authoritie therof, That all covenous or fraudulent alienations or conveyances of lands, tenements or any hereditaments ſhall be of no validitie to defeat any man from due debts or legacyes, or from any juſt title, claim or poſſeſſion of that which is ſo fraudulently conveyed.

2 For avoiding all fraudulent conveyances and that every man may know what eſtate or intereſt other men may have in any houſes, lands or other hereditamēts they are to deal in, it is therfore ordered by the authoritie of this Court;

That after the end of October 1640 no morgage, bargain, ſale, or graunt made of any houſes, lands, rents or other hereditaments where the Graunter remains in poſſeſſion, ſhall be of force againſt other perſons except the Graunter and his Heirs, unleſs the ſame be acknowledged before ſome Magiſtrate & recorded as is heerafter expreſſed: and that no ſuch bargain, ſale or graunt already made, in way of morgage, where the Graunter remains

C

nor unburied 12 hours &c

Conſtable correct or get another

Forr: Juriſd: Offendr conveyed fro Cōſtable to Cōſt.

Hue-&-cries purſued Conſt: may put forth Hu-&-cries.

apprehend divers offenders

ſearch for thē

cōmit to cuſtodie.

All to aſſiſt Conſt:

on penaltie of ſo ſs.

wilful negl: & 40 ſs.

Conſt: ſtaffe.

Magiſtr: Conſt: &c to rvſe hue-&-crie ō Capit: offences on penal: of 40 ſs.

Invalid.

ules recorded

within a mōth

or 3 months

Graunter refuſe to ackn: impriſoned.

recorded in ẏ Shire in a mō:

& certified to ẏ Secr: in 6 months.

remains in poſſeſſion ſhall be of force againſt other but the Graunter of his Heirs, except the ſame ſhall be entred as is heerafter expreſſed within one month after the date aforementioned: if the partie be within this Juriſdiction or elſe within three months after he ſhal return. And if any ſuch Graunter being required by the Grauntee, his Heirs or Aſſignes to make a acknowledgment of any graunt, ſale, bargain or morgage by him made ſhall refuſe ſo to doe, it ſhall be in the power of any Magiſtrate to ſend for the partie ſo refuſing, & commit him to priſon without *Bayle* or *Main-prize*, untill he ſhall acknowledge the ſame, and the Grauntee is to enter his *caution* with the Recorder, and this ſhall ſave his intereſt in the mean time. And if it be doubtfull whether it be the deed and graunt of the partie, he ſhal be bound with Suerties to the next court of Aſſiſtants & the *caution* ſhal remain good as aforeſaid. And for recording of all ſuch graunts, ſales, bargains or morgages; it is further ordered, that there ſhall be one appointed in everie Shire choſen by each court of the ſaid Shires for Recorders to enter all ſuch graunts, ſales, bargains, morgages of houſes, lands, rents and other hereditamēts as aforeſaid together with the names of Graunter and Grauntee, thing and eſtate graunted & the date therof. All which entries ſhall be certified unto the Recorder or Secretarie for the Generall Court within ſix months from time to time. [1640] [1641]

*Councill.*

In caſe impor: a Gēeral court called by the Governour

ſtanding Coūcil how to be called How many may act for impreſſing men.

& all other things.

*This Court conſidering how the weighty affairs of this Juriſdiction whether they concern this peculiarly or have reference to the reſt of our confœderated Colonies may be duly and ſpeedily tranſacted in the vacancy of the Generall Court for the ſatisfaction of the Commiſſioners, in reſpect of the weighty and ſodain occaſions which may be then in hand, doth heerby expreſſe and declare,* That the Generall Court ought to be called by the Governour, when the importancy of the buſines doth require it, and that time and opportunitie will ſafely admit the ſame, and that all other neceſſary matters are to be ordered and diſpatched by the major part of the Council of the Common-wealth; & therfore to that end letters ſignifying, breifly, the buſines and the time and place of meeting for conſultation ought to be ſent unto the Aſſiſtants. Alſo it is heerby declared, that ſeven of the ſaid Aſſiſtants meeting, the Governour or Deputy Governour being one is a ſufficient Aſſembly to act, by impreſſing of ſoldiers or otherwiſe as need ſhall be. And in caſe of extream and urgent neceſſitie, when indeavours are reaſonably uſed to call together the Aſſiſtants and the buſines will not admit delay, then the acts of ſo many as do aſſemble are to be accounted, and are accounted valid, & ſufficient. Alſo it is intended that the generall words aforementioned contein in them power to impreſſe & ſend forth ſoldiers, and all manner of victuails, veſſels at ſea, carriages and all other neceſſaries, and to ſend *warrants* to the Treaſurer to pay for them. [1645]

*Courts.*

4 courts of Aſſiſtants

4 Coū: courts at Boſton

for all civil cauſ: & crim: not extend: to life &c

4 quar: Courts in Eſſex.

*For the better adminiſtration of juſtice and eaſing the Countrie of unneceſſary charge and travells: it is ordered by this Court and Authoritie therof;*

That there ſhal be four Quarter Courts of Aſſiſtants yearly kept by the Governour, or Deputy Gover: and the reſt of the Magiſtrates, the firſt of them on the firſt third day *(viz: tuisday)* in the fourth month called *June*: the ſecond on the firſt third day of the ſeventh month: the third on the firſt third day of the tenth mōth: the fourth on the firſt third day of the firſt month called *March*. Alſo there be four County Courts held at *Boſton*, by ſuch of the Magiſtrates as ſhall reſide in, or neer the ſame, *viz:* by any five, four or three of them, who ſhall have power to aſſemble together upō the laſt fift day of the eight, eleveneth, ſecond & fift months everie year, and there to hear & determin all civil cauſes & criminal, not extending to life, member or baniſhment according to the courſe of the court of Aſſiſtants, & to ſummon Juries out of the neighbour towns, & the Marſhall & other Officers ſhall give attendance there as at other Courts. And it is further ordered that there ſhall be four Quarter Courts kept yearly by the Magiſtrates of Eſſex, with ſuch other perſons of worth as ſhal frō time to time be appointed by the General Court; at the nominatiō of the towns in that Shire by orderly agreemēt amōg thēſelves, to be joyned in Commiſſion with them ſo that with the Magiſtrates they be five in all

in all and so that no Court be kept without one Magistrate at the least : and so any three
of the Commissioners aforesaid may keep Court in the absence of the rest : yet none of
all the Magistrates are excluded from any of these Courts who can, and please to attend
the same. And the Generall Court to appoint from time to time, which of the said
Magistrates shall specially belong to everie of the said Courts. Two of these Quarter
Courts shall be kept at *Salem*, the other at *Ipswitch*. The first, the last third day of the
week in the seventh month at *Ipswitch*. The second at *Salem* the last third day of the
tenth month. The third at *Ipswitch* the last third day of the first month. The fourth
the last third day of the fourth month at *Salem*. All and every which Courts shall be
holden by the Magistrates of *Salem* and *Ipswitch* with the rest of that County or so many
of them as shall attend the same ; but no Jurie men shal be warned from *Ipswitch* to Salem nor from *Salem* to *Ipswitch*. Also there shall be a Grand Jurie at either place, once a
year. Which Courts shal have the same power in civil and criminal causes as the courts
of Assistants have (at *Boston*) except tryalls for life, lims or banishment, which are who-
ly reserved unto the courts of Assistants. The like libertie for County courts and tryall of
causes is graunted to the Shire town of *Cambridge* for the County of *Midlesex*, as *Essex*
hath, to be holden by the Magistrates of *Midlesex* & *Suffolk* & such other men of worth
as shall be nominated and chosen as aforesaid, one of which Courts shall be holden on
the last third day of the eight month, and another on the last third day of the second
month from year to year. And the like libertie for County Courts and tryall of causes
is graunted to the County of *Norfolk* to be holden at *Salisburie* on the last third day of the
second month ; and another at *Hampton* on such day as the General Court shall appoint
to be kept in each place from time to time. And if any shal finde himselfe greived with
the sentence of any the said County courts he may appeal to the next court of Assistants.
Provided he put in sufficiēt caution according to law. Lastly, it is ordered by the Authoritie aforesaid that all causes brought to the courts of Assistants by way of appeal, and o-
ther causes specially belonging to the said courts, shall be first determined from time to
time: & that causes of divorce shall be tryed only in the said court of Assistants. [1635
1636 1639 1641 1642]

2 *For the more speedy dispatch of all causes which shall concern Strangers, who cannot
stay to attend the ordinary Courts of justice, It is ordered by this Court and Authoritie therof ;*

That the Governour or Deputy Governour with any two other Magistrates, or
when the Governour or Deputy Governour cannot attend it, that any three Magistrates
shall have power to hear and determin by a Jurie of twelve men, or otherwise as is used
in other Courts, all causes civil and criminal triable in County Courts, which shall arise
between such Strangers, or wherin any such Stranger shall be a partie. And all records of such proceedings shall be transmitted to the Records of the Court of Assistants,
to be entred as tryalls in other Courts, all which shall be at the charge of the parties,
as the Court shall determin, so as the Country be no wayes charged by such courts.
[1639]

3 *For the electing of our Governour, Deputy Governour, Assistants and other generall
Officers upon the day or dayes appointed by our Pattent to hold our yearly Court being the
last fourth day of the week (viz: Wednesday) of every Easter Term ; it is solemnly and
unanimously decreed and established,*

That henceforth the Freemen of this Jurisdiction shal either in person or by proxie
without any *Summons* attend & consummate the Elections, at which time also they shal
send their Deputies with full power to consult of and determin such matters as concern
the welfare of this Common-wealth : from which General Court no Magistrate or Deputy shall depart or be discharged without the consent of the major part both of Magistrates and Deputies, during the first four dayes of the first Session therof, under the
penaltie of one hundred pounds for everie such default on either part. And for the after

C 2                                    Sessions

---

*Marginal notes (right column):*

not kept with-
out one Magist
rate at le. &
Gen: court
appoint w Ma-
gistr: to each
Court

7 mon: at Ips-
witch.
10 mō: at Salē
&c:

for all civil
& crim: causes
exc: cases of
life, lims, or
banishment.
Court at Cam-
bridge for
Midlesex.

Courts at Sa-
lisburie and
Hampton for
Norfolk

Appeal to
court of Assist

Divorce.

Courts extra-
ordinary.

at partyes
charge

Courts of E-
lection wout
Summons.

No member
of Court to
depart wout
licence.

Seffions, if any be, the Deputies for *Dover* are at libertie whether to attēd or not. [1643]

4 For a*fmuch as after long experience wee finde divers inconveniences in the manner of our proceeding in Courts by Magiftrates and Deputies fitting together, and account it wifedome to follow the laudable practice of other States, who have layd ground works for government and order for iffuing bufines of greateft and higheft confequence: it is therfore ordered by this Court and Authoritie therof,*

Gen: Court.

That henceforth the Magiftrates may fit and act bufines by themfelves, by drawing up Bills and Orders which they fhall fee good in their wifedom, which having agreed upon, they may prefent them to the Deputies to be confidered of, how good and wholefom fuch orders are for the Countrie & accordingly to give their affent or diffent. The Deputies in like manner fitting apart by themfelves and confulting about fuch orders and laws as they in their difcretion and experience fhall finde meet for the common good: which agreed upon by them they may prefent to the Magiftrates who having ferioufly confidered of them may manifeft their confent or diffent therto. And when any Orders have paffed the approbation of both Magiftrates and Deputies, then to be ingroffed: which in the laft day of this Court or Seffions fhal be deliberately read over. Provided alfo that all matters of Judicature which this Court fhall take cognifance of, fhall be iffued in like manner (unles the Court upon fome particular occafion or bufines agree otherwife). [1644]

*Magiftrates act apart.*

*Bils read over ẏ laft day of the Seffion. Matter of Judicature*

### Criminal caufes.

It is ordered by this court & Authoritie therof, That everie man that is to anfwer for any criminal caufe, whether he be in prifon or under *Bayle* his caufe fhall be heard and determined at the next Court that hath proper cognifance therof and may be done without prejudice of juftice. [1641] *See Courts, Lib: com: Punifhment, Torture.*

*heard next Court*

### Crueltie.

It is ordered by this Court and Authoritie therof; That no man fhall exercife any tyrany or cruelty towards any bruit creatures which are ufually kept for the ufe of man. [1641]

### Damages pretended.

It is ordered by this Court and Authoritie therof; That no man in any Sute or Action againft another fhall falfly pretend great damages or debts to vex his adverfary, and if it fhall appear any doth fo, the Court fhall have power to fet a reafonable fine on his head. [1641]

*Finable.*

### Death untimely.

It is ordered by this Court and Authoritie therof; That whenfoever any perfon fhall come to any very fodain, untimely or unatural death, fome Affiftant or the Conftable of that town fhall forthwith fummon a Jurie of twelve difcreet men to inquire of the caufe and manner of their death, who fhall prefent a true verdict therof, to fome neer Affiftant, or to the next court (to be holden for that Shire) upon their oath. [1641]

*Tryed by inqueft.*

### Deeds and writings.

It is ordered by this court and Authoritie therof; That no conveyance, deed or promife whatfoever fhall be of validitie, if it be gotten by illegal violence, imprifonment, threatening or any kinde of forcible compulfion, called *Dures.* [1641]

*Invalid.*

### Deputies for the Generall Court.

For eafing the body of Freemen now increafing, and better difpatching the bufines of Generall Courts, It is ordered and by this Court declared;

That henceforth it fhall be lawfull for the Freemen of everie Plantation to choofe their Deputies before every Generall Court, to confer of, and prepare fuch publick bufines as by them fhall be thought fit to confider of at the next General court. And that fuch perfons as fhall be heerafter fo deputed by the Freemen of the feveral Plantations to deal on their behalfe in the publick affairs of the Common-wealth, fhall have the full power and voices of all the faid Freemen derived to them for the making and eftablifhing of Laws, graunting of lands, and to deal in all other affairs of the Cōmon-wealth wherin

*Towns choofe Deputies. their power before the Court*

*their power in Court*

wherin the Freemen have to doe: the matter of election of Magiftrates and other Officers only excepted wherin every Freeman is to give his own voice. [1634]

2 *Forafmuch as through the bleffing of God the number of towns are much increafed, It is therfore ordered and by this Court enacted;*

That henceforth no town fhall fend more then two Deputies to the General Court; though the number of Freemen in any town be more then twenty. And that all towns which have not to the number of twenty Freemen fhall fend but one Deputy, & fuch towns as have not ten Freemen fhall fend none, but fuch Freemen fhall vote with the next town in the choice of their Deputie or Deputies til this Court take further order. [1636 1638]

3 It is ordered by this Court and Authoritie therof, That when the Deputyes for feverall towns are met together before, or at any General court, it fhall be lawfull for them or the major part of them to hear and determin any difference that may arife about the election of any of their members, and to order things amongft themfelves that may concern the well ordering of their body. And that heerafter the Deputies for the General court fhall be elected by papers as the Governour is chofen. [1634 1635]

4 It is ordered by this Court and Authoritie therof; That the Freemen of any Shire or town have liberty to choofe fuch Deputies for the General court either in their own Shire, Town, or elfewhere, as they judge fitteft, fo be it they be Freemen and inhabiting within this Jurisdiction. And becaufe wee cannot forefee what variety and weight of occafions may fall into future confideration, & what counfells we may ftand in need of: wee decree that the Deputies to attend the General court in the behalfe of the Country fhall not at any time be ftated and enacted but from court to court, or at the moft but for one year, that the Countrie may have an annual liberty to doe in that cafe what is moft behoofefull for the beft welfare therof. [1641]

### Diftreffe.

It is ordered by this Court and Authoritie therof, That no mans corn or hay that is in the field or upon the cart, nor his garden-ftuffe, nor any thing fubject to prefent decay, fhall be taken in any diftreffe, unles he that takes it doth prefently beftow it where it may not be imbeazled nor fuffer fpoyl or decay, or give fecuritie to fatisfie the worth therof if it comes to any harm. [1641]

### Dowries.

*Forafmuch as no provifion hath yet been made for any certein maintainance for Wives after the death of their Husbands, be it ordered and enacted by this prefent Court and Authoritie therof;*

That every married Woman (living with her Husband in this Jurisdicton or other where abfent from him with his confent or through his meer default, or inevitable providence, or in cafe of divorce where fhe is the innocent partie) that fhal not before marriage be eftated by way of joynture in fome houfes, lands, tenements or other hereditaments for term of her life, fhall immediatly after the death of her Husband have right and intereft by way of *dower,* in, and to one third part of all fuch houfes, lands, tenemets, rents and hereditaments as her faid Husband was feized of, to his own ufe, either in *poffeffion, reverfion* or *remainder* in any eftate of inheritance (or *franc-tenement* not then determined) at any time during the marriage to have and injoy for term of her natural life according to the eftate of fuch Husband free, and freely difcharged of and from all titles, debts, rents, charges, judgements, executions and other incumbrances whatfoever had, made, or fuffered by her faid Husband during the faid marriage between them; or by any other perfon claiming by, from, or under him otherwife then by any act or confent of fuch Wife, as the laws of this Court fhall ratefie and allow: and if the Heir of the Husband or other perfon interrefted, fhall not within one month after lawfull demand made, affigne and fet

C 3 out to

---

Right margin notes:

matter of election except:

Nuber of Dep: for each town.

Deputies may fetle differ: about elect: of Deputies & order their own body.

Whence chofen. How qualified.

Stated but for one year at moft.

Secured.

What wives are dowable

wherof.

for life.

free of incumbrance.

How to be assigned: with costs & damages. Limitation

out to such widow, her just third part with conveniencie or to her satisfaction according to the intent of this Law, then upō a *writt* of *dower* in the court of that Shire where the said houses, lands, tenements or other hereditaments shall lye; or in the court of Assistants (if the same lye in several Shires) her *dower* or third part shal be assigned her to be set forth in severall by mets and bounds, by such persons as the same Court shall appoint for that purpose, with all costs and damages susteined. Provided alwayes that this Law shall not extend to any houses lands, tenements or other hereditaments solde or conveyed away, by any husband *bona fide* for valuable consideration, before the last of the ninth month now last past. And it is farther inacted that everie such Wife as is before expressed immediatly after the death of her Husband, shal have interest in, and unto one third part of all such monie, goods and chattels, real and personal of what kinde soever as her Husband shall dye possessed of (so much as shall be sufficient for the discharge of his Funerall and just debts being first deducted) to be allowed and set out to her as is heer before appointed for her Dowrie. Provided alwayes that every such widow so endowed as aforesaid shall not commit or suffer any strip or wast, but shal maintain all such houses, fences and inclosures as shall be assigned to her for her Dowrie, and shall leave the same in good and sufficient repairations in all points. [1647]

Third of personal estate

restreint from wast.

## *Drovers.*

Liberty.

It is ordered by this Court and Authoritie therof; That if any man shall have occasion to lead or drive cattle from place to place that is far off, so that they be weary or hungrie, or fall sick or lame, it shall be lawfull to rest and refresh them for a competent time in any open place that is not corn, meadow, or inclosed for some particular use. [1641]

## *Ecclesiasticall:*

1 All the people of God within this Jurisdiction who are not in a Church way and be orthodox in judgement and not scandalous in life shall have full libertie to gather themselves into a Church estate, provided they doe it in a christian way with due observation of the rules of Christ revealed in his word. Provided also that the General Court doth not, nor will heerafter approve of any such companyes of men as shall joyne in any pretended way of Church fellowship unles they shall acquaint the Magistrates and the Elders of the neighbour Churches where they intend to joyn, & have their approbation therin.

Approbation.

2 And it is farther ordered, that no person being a member of any Church which shal be gathered without the approbation of the Magistrates and the said Churches shal be admitted to the Freedom of this Common-wealth.

Non-appoba:

3 Everie Church hath free liberty to exercise all the Ordinances of God according to the rules of the Scripture.

Ordinances

4 Everie Church hath free libertie of election and ordination of all her Officers from time to time. Provided they be able, pious and orthodox.

Officers.

5 Everie Church hath also free libertie of admission, recommendation, dismission & expulsion or deposall of their Officers and members upon due cause, with free exercise of the disciplin and censures of Christ according to the rules of his word.

Members.

6 No injunction shall be put upon any Church, church Officer or member in point of doctrine, worship or disciplin, whether for substance or circumstance besides the institutions of the Lord.

No humane Ordinances.

7 Everie Church of Christ hath freedom to celebrate dayes of Fasting and prayer and of Thanksgiving according to the word of God.

Fasts & Feasts

8 The Elders of churches also have libertie to meet monthly, quarterly or otherwise in convenient numbers and places, for conference and consultations about christian and church questions and occasions.

Elders meet:

9 All Churches also have libertie to deal with any their members in a church way that are in the hands of justice, so it be not to retard and hinder the course therof.

Members ūder civil justice.

10 Everie

10 Everie Church hath libertie to deal with any Magistrate, Deputy of court, or other Officer whatsoever that is a member of theirs, in a church way in case of apparent and just offence, given in their places, so it be done with due observance and respect.    *civil Officers.*

11 Wee also allow private meetings for edification in Religion amongst christians of all sorts of people so it be without just offence, both for number, time, place and other circumstances.    *Private meet:*

12 *For the preventing and removing of errour and offence that may grow and spread in any of the Churches in this Jurisdiction, and for the preserving of truth & peace in the severall Churches within themselves, and for the maintainance and exercise of brotherly cōmunion amongst all the Churches in the country.*

It is allowed and ratified by the authoritie of this Court, as a lawfull libertie of the Churches of Christ, that once in every month of the year (when the season will bear it) it shall be lawfull for the Ministers and Elders of the Churches neer adjoyning, together with any other of the Brethren, with the consent of the Churches, to assemble by course in everie several church one after another, to the intent, that after the preaching of the word, by such a Minister as shal be requested therto, by the Elders of the Church where the Assemby is held, the rest of the day may be spent in publick christian conference, about the discussing and resolving of any such doubts & cases of conscience concerning matter of doctrine, or worship, or government of the Church as shall be propounded by any of the Brethren of that Church; with leave also to any other Brother to propound his objections, or answers, for further satisfaction according to the word of God. Provided that the whole action be guided and moderated by the Elders of the Church where the Assembly is held, or by such others as they shall appoint. And that nothing be concluded & imposed by way of Authoritie from one, or more Churches, upon another, but only by way of brotherly conference & consultations, that the truth may be searched out to the satisfying of every mans conscience in the sight of God according to his word. And because such an Assemblie and the work therof cannot be duly attended if other Lectures be held the same week, it is therfore agreed with the consent of the Churches, that in what week such an Assembly is held all the Lectures in all the neighbouring Churches for the week dayes shall be forborne, that so the publick service of Christ in this Assembly may be transacted with greater diligence & attention. [1641]

*Monthly meetings.*

*For preaching & conference*

*Moderators.*

*No Presbyterial authority over Chur:*

*no Lectures ye week.*

13 *Forasmuch as the open contempt of Gods word and Messengers therof is the desolating sinne of civil States and Churches and that the preaching of the word by those whom God doth send, is the chief ordinary means ordained of God for the converting, edifying and saving the soules of the Elect through the presence and power of the Holy-Ghost, therunto promised: and that the ministry of the word, is set up by God in his Churches, for those holy ends: and according to the respect or contempt of the same and of those whom God hath set apart for his own work & imployment, the weal or woe of all Christian States is much furthered and promoted; it is therfore ordered and decreed,*

That if any christian (so called) within this Jurisdiction shall contemptuously behave himselfe toward the Word preached or the Messengers therof called to dispense the same in any Congregation; when he doth faithfully execute his Service and Office therin, according to the will and word of God, either by interrupting him in his preaching, or by charging him falsely with any errour which he hath not taught in the open face of the Church; or like a son of *Korah* cast upon his true doctrine or himselfe any reproach, to the dishonour of the Lord Jesus who hath sent him and to the disparagement of that his holy Ordinance, and making Gods wayes contemptible and ridiculous: that everie such person or persons (whatsoever censure the Church may passe) shall for the first scandall be convented and reproved openly by the Magistrate at some Lecture, and bound to their good behaviour. And if a second time they break forth into the like contemptuous carriages, they shall either pay five pounds to the publick Treasurie; or stand two hours openly upon a block or stool, four foot high

*contempt of the word &c*

*first offence openly reproved &c: Second offen:*

high on a lecture day with a paper fixed on his breast, written in Capital letters [AN O-
PEN AND OBSTINATE CONTEMNER OF GODS HOLY ORDINANCES]
that others may fear and be ashamed of breaking out into the like wickednes. [1646]

14 It is ordered and decreed by this Court and Authoritie therof ; That wheresoever
the ministry of the word is established according to the order of the Gospell throughout
this Jurisd.ction every person shall duly resort and attend therunto respectively upon the
Lords days & upon such publick Fast dayes, & dayes of Thankfgiving as are to be generally kept by the appointmēt of Authoritie: & if any person withī this Jurisdictiō shal
without just and necessarie cause withdraw himselfe frō hearing the publick ministry of
the word after due meanes of conviction used, he shall forfeit for his absence from everie such publick meeting five shillings .      All such offences to be heard and determined
by any one Magistrate or more from time to time . [1646]

Absence from church Attem:

fined 5 ss

15 *Forasmuch as the peace and prosperity of Churches and members therof as well as ci-*
*vil Rights & Liberties are carefully to be maintained, it is ordered by this Court & decreed,*
That the civil Authoritie heer established hath power and liberty to see the peace, ordinances and rules of Christ be observed in everie Church according to his word.   As also
to deal with any church-member in a way of civil justice notwithstanding any church
relation, office, or interest ; so it be done in a civil and not in an ecclesiastical way.   Nor
shall any church censure degrade or depose any man from any civil dignity, office or authoritie he shall have in the Common-wealth. [1641]

Civil author: may preserve peace in chu: Punish chur: members nor shal chur: cēse: disanul civil dignity.

16 *Forasmuch as there are many Inhabitants in divers towns, who leave their several*
*habitations and therby draw much of the in-come of their estates into other towns wherby*
*the ministry is much neglected, it is therfore ordered by this Court and the authoritie therof ;*
That from henceforth all lands, cattle and other estates of any kinde whatsoever, shall be
lyable to be rated to all cōmon charges whatsoever, either for the Church, Town or Cōmon-wealth in the same place where the estate is from time to time .     And to the end
there may be a convenient habitation for the use of the ministry in everie town in this Ju-
risd.ction to remain to posterity. It is decreed by the authoritie of this Court that where
the major part of the Inhabitants (according to the order of regulating valid town act)
shall graunt, build, or purchase such habitation it shall be good in law, and the particular sum upon each person assessed by just rate, shal be duly paid according as in other cases of town rates .     Provided alwayes that such graunt, deed of purchase and the deed
of gift therupon to the use of a present preaching Elder and his next successour and so
from time to time to his successors : be entred in the town book and acknowledged before a Magistrate, and recorded in the Shire court. [1647] *See charges publ: sec: 3.*

What is rateable for the ministry.

Ministers hous

to go to successors.

recorded.

## Elections.

It is ordered by this Court and Authoritie therof : That for the yearly choosing of
Assistants for the time to come in stead of papers the Freemen shall use indian corn and
beans.   the indian corn to manifest election, the beans for blanks.    And that if any
Freeman shall put in more then one indian corn or bean for the choise or refusal of any
publick Officer, he shall forteit for everie such offence ten pounds.   And that any man
that is not free or otherwse hath not libertie of voting, putting in any vote shal forteit the
like sum of ten pounds . [1643]

Election by indian corn & beans.  no man put in above one, on penal: of 10 li.

no non-Frem: any, on like penaltie.

2 *For the preventing of many inconveniences that otherwise may arise upon the yearly*
*day of Election, and that the work of that day may be the more orderly, easily and speedily*
*issued, it is ordered by this Court and the authoritie therof.*

That the Freemen in the several towns and villages within this Jurisdiction, shall
this next year from time to time either in person or by proxie sealed up, make all their e-
lections, by papers, indian corn and beans as heerafter is expressed , to be taken , sealed
up, & sent to the court of Election as this order appoints, the Governour, Deputie Governour, Major Generall, Treasurer, Secretary and Cōmissioners for the united Colonies
to be chosen by writing, open or once folded, not twisted or rolled up, that so they may
                be

Election by proxies how to be carried

be the sooner and surer perused : and all the Assistants to be chosen by indian corn and beans, the indian corn to manifest election as in *Sect:* 1 : and for such small villages as come not in person and that send no Deputies to the Court, the Constable of the said village, together with two or three of the chiefe Freemen shall receive the votes of the rest of their Freemen, and deliver them together with their own sealed up to the Deputie or Deputies for the next town, who shall carefully convey the same unto the said Court of Election. [1647]

3 *Forasmuch as the choice of Assistants in case of supply is of great concernment, and with all care and circumspection to be attended ; It is therefore ordered by this Court and Authoritie therof,*

That when any Assistants are to be supplyed, the Deputies for the General Court shall give notice to their Constables or Select men to call together their Freemen in their severall towns : to give in their votes unto the number of seven persons, or as the General Court shall direct, who shall then and there appoint one to carrie them sealed up unto their Shire towns upon the last fourth day of the week in the first month from time to time ; which persons for each town so assembled shall appoint one for each Shire to carrie them unto *Boston* the second third day of the second month there to be opened before two Magistrates . And those seven or other number agreed upon as aforesaid, that have most votes shall be the men which shall be nominated at the court of Election for Assistants as aforesaid . Which persons the Agents for each Shire shall forthwith signifie to the Constables of all their several towns in writing under their hands with the number of votes for each person : all which the said Constables shall forthwith signifie to their Freemen . And as any hath more votes then other so shall they be put to vote . [1647]

4 It is decreed and by this Court declared That it is the constant libertie of the Freemen of this Jurisdiction to choose yearly at the court of Election out of the Freemen, all the general Officers of this Jurisdiction, and if they please to discharge them at the court of Election by way of vote they may doe it without shewing cause . But if at any other General Court, we hold it due justice that the reason therof be alledged and proved . By general Officers we mean our Governour, Deputy Governour, Assistants, Treasurer, General of our wars, our Admirall at sea, Commissioners for the united-Colonies and such others as are, or heerafter may be of the like general nature . [1641] *See courts Sect:* 3.

### Escheats.

It is ordered by this Court and Authoritie therof, That where no Heir or Owner of houses, lands, tenements, goods or chattels can be found : they shall be seized to the publick Treasurie till such Heirs or owners shall make due claim therto, unto whom they shall be restored upon just and reasonable terms . [1646]

### Farms.

It is ordered by this Court and Authoritie therof, That all Farms which are within the bounds of any town shall henceforth be of the same town in which they lye, except *Meadford.* [1641] *See militarie . see watches.*

### Fayrs & Markets.

It is ordered by the Authoritie of this Court that there shall henceforth be a Market kept at *Boston* in the county of *Suffolk* upô the fift day of the week from time to time. And at *Salem* in the county of *Essex* upon the fourth day of the week from time to time. And at *Lyn* on the third day of the week from time to time . And at *Charls-town* in the county of *Middlesex* upon the sixt day of the week from time to time . It is also ordered and heerby graunted unto *Salem* afore-mentioned to have two Fayrs in a year on the last fourth day of the third month and the last fourth day of the seventh month from year to year . Also *Water-town* in the County of *Middlesex* is graunted two Fayrs on the first sixt day of the fourth month & the first sixt day of the seventh month from year to year . Also *Dorchester* in the County of *Suffolk* is graunted two Fayrs on the third

D

fourth day of the first month and the last fourth day of the eight month from year to year [1633 1634 1636 1638]

### Ferries.

*For setling all common ferries in a right course both for the Passengers and Owners, it is ordered by this Court and authoritie therof;*

That whosoever hath a Ferry graunted upon any passage shall have the sole libertie for transporting passengers from the place where such Ferrie is graunted, to any other ferrie-place where ferrie-boats use to land, and any ferrie-boat that shall land passengers at any other Ferrie may not take passengers from thence if the ferrie-boat of the place be ready. Provided this order shall not prejudice the libertie of any that do use to passe in their own or neighbours *cannooes* or boats to their ordinary labour or busines. Also Ferrimen are allowed to take double pay at such common Ferries after day light is done, and those that make not present pay, being required, shall give their names in writing or a pawn to the Ferriman, or else he may complain of such before a Magistrate to get satisfaction. And it is ordered that all the Magistrates and such as are, or from time to time shall be chosen to serve as Deputies of the General Court, with their necessary attendants *viz:* a man and a horse at all times, during the time of their being Magistrates or Deputies [and not their whole families] shall be passage-free over all Ferries. Provided where Ferries are appropriated to any, or rented out & so be out of the Countries hands their passage shall be paid by the Countrie. And the Ferrimen of *Charls-River* are allowed for the passage of the Magistrates, Deputies, Grand and petty Juriemen, prisoners, Keepers and Marshals, by agreement with them six pounds *per annum* to be paid by the Treasurer.

*And wheras men doe passe over the common Ferries in great danger oftentimes, and the Ferrimen excuse themselves by the importunitie of passengers and want of law to inable them to keep due order touching passengers, its therfore neerby farther ordered;*

That no person shall presse or enter into any ferrie-boat contrary to the will of the Ferriman or of the most of the passengers first entred upon payn of ten shillings for every such attempt: and that everie Ferriman that shall permit and allow any person to come into his boat against the will of any of the Magistrates or Deputies or any of the Elders shipped in such boat or the greater part of the passengers in the said boat, shall forfeit for everie person so admitted or received against such their will so declared the sum of twentie shillings. And it shall be in the power of any of the Ferrimen to keep out or put out of his boat any person that shall presse, enter into, or stay in any such ferrie-boat contrary to this Order. And it is farther ordered that all persons shall be received into such ferrie-boats according to their comming, first or last, only all Publick persons or such as goe upon publick or urgent occasions, as Phisitians, Chirurgeons and Midwives and such other as are called to woemens labours, such shall be transported with the first. [1641 1644 1646 1647] *See Colledge.*

### Fines.

*Wheras divers persons indebted to the Countrie for publick Rates, & others for Fines who for avoiding payment somtime sell their houses and lands, and send away their goods to other Plantations, it is therfore ordered by the authoritie of this Court,*

That the Treasurer shall graunt *Warrant* to the Marshall to attach the bodyes of such persons, & keep them til they make satisfaction; and all such persons as are to pay any fines if they have not lands or goods to be distreined shall have their bodyes attached to make satisfaction. Provided that any Court of Assistants or County Court may discharge any such person from imprisonment if they shall finde them indeed unable to make satisfaction. [1638]

### Fyre.

It is ordered by this Court and the Authoritie therof, that whosoever shall kindle any fyres in woods or grounds lying in common or inclosed, so as the same shall run into such corn grounds or inclosures; before the tenth of the first month or after the last of the second month, or on the last day of the week, or on the Lords day shall pay all damages and

---

*Marginal notes:*

Priviledge of Ferries.

Men may pass in own or neighbours boat. Double pay in the night How Ferrymē may recover their pay. Magistr: and Dep: passage free:

payd by the Countrie for them & others 6 li. per an.

Secur: passen:

Ferriman's power.

men shall passe as they come exc: publick persons &c:

where no est: is foud person attached.

The court may disch: from prison.

In what cases he ȳ kindles fire shal pay all damages

and half ſo much for a Fine , or if not able to pay then to be corporally puniſhed by *Warrant* from one Magiſtrate or the next County Court as the offence ſhall deſerve, not exceeding twenty ſtripes for one offence . Provided that any man may kindle fyre in his own ground at any time , ſo as no damage come therby either to the Country or any particular perſon . And whoſoever ſhall wittingly and willingly burn or deſtroy any frame, timber hewed, ſawn or ryven , heaps of wood, charcoal, corn, hay, ſtraw, hemp or flax he ſhall pay double damages .

and be fined or corporally puniſhed

Wilfull burning timber, corn &c: double damage

### Fiſh. Fiſher-men.

UPON the petition of the Inhabitants of Marble-head *this Court doth heerby declare that howſoever it hath been an allowed cuſtom for forreign fiſhermen to make uſe of ſuch Harbours and Grounds in this Countrie as have not been inhabited by Engliſh men, and to take timber and wood at their pleaſure for all their occaſions , yet in theſe parts which are now poſſeſſed and the lands diſpoſed in proprietie unto ſeverall towns and perſons and that by his* Majeſtyes *graunt under the Great Seal of England ,*

It is not now lawfull for any perſon either Fiſherman or other , either Forreiner or of this Countrie to enter upon the lands ſo appropriated to any town or perſon , or to take any wood or timber in any ſuch place without the licence of ſuch town or Proprietor : and if any perſon ſhall treſpaſſe heerin the Town or Proprietor ſo injured may take their remedie by Action at law , or may preſerve their goods or other interreſt by oppoſing lawfull force againſt ſuch unjuſt violence . Provided that it ſhall be lawfull for ſuch Fiſhermen as ſhall be imployed by any Inhabitants in this Juriſdiction in the ſeverall ſeaſons of the year to make uſe of any of our Harbours and ſuch lands as are neer adjoyning, for the drying of their fiſh or other needfull occaſions , as alſo to have ſuch timber or fire-wood as they ſhall have neceſſary uſe of for their fiſhing ſeaſons where it may be ſpared , ſo as they make due ſatisfaction for the ſame to ſuch Town or Proprietor. [1646]

Forr: Fiſhermens cuſtom for timber &c:

not allowed.

Lib: for our own Fiſhermē

upon due ſatisfaction.

### Forgerie.

IT is ordered by this Court and Authoritie therof , That if any perſon ſhall forge any Deed or conveyance, Teſtament, Bond, Bill, Releaſ, Acquittance, Letter of Attourny or any writing to pervert equitie and juſtice , he ſhall ſtand in the *Pillory* three ſeverall Lecture dayes and render double damages to the partie wronged and alſo be diſſabled to give any evidence or verdict to any Court or Magiſtrate . [1646]

### Fornication

IT is ordered by this Court and Authoritie therof , That if any man ſhall commit Fornication with any ſingle woman , they ſhall be puniſhed either by enjoyning to Marriage , or Fine, or corporall puniſhment, or all or any of theſe as the judges in the courts of Aſſiſtants ſhall appoint moſt agreeable to the word of God . And this Order to continue till the Court take further order . [1642]

### Freemen, Non-Freemen.

WHERAS *there are within this Juriſdiction many members of Churches who to exempt themſelves from all publick ſervice in the Common-wealth will not come in , to be made Freemen , is is therfore ordered by this Court and the Authoritie therof ,*

That all ſuch members of Churches in the ſeverall towns within this Juriſdiction ſhall not be exempted from ſuch publick ſervice as they are from time to time choſen to by the Freemen of the ſeverall towns ; as Conſtables, Jurors, Select-men and Surveyors of high-wayes . And if any ſuch perſon ſhall refuſe to ſerve in, or take upon him any ſuch Office being legally choſen therunto , he ſhall pay for every ſuch refuſall ſuch Fine as the town ſhall impoſe , not exceeding twenty ſhillings as Freemen are lyable to in ſuch caſes . [1647]

Who are compellable to publ: ſervices

### Fugitives , Strangers.

IT is ordered by this Court and Authoritie therof , That if any people of other nations profeſſing the true Chiſtian Religion ſhall flee to us from the tyranie or oppreſſion of their perſecutors , or from Famine , Wars, or the like neceſſarie and

D 2

compulſarie

compulsarie cause , they shall be entertained and succoured amongst us according to that power and prudence God shall give us . [1641]

## Gaming.

*Harboured.*

UPON *complaint of great disorder by the use of the game called* Shuffle-board, *in houses of common entertainment , wherby much pretious time is spent unfruitfully and much waft of wine and beer occasioned , it is therfore ordered and enacted by the Authoritie of this Court ;*

*Shuffleboard*

That no person shall henceforth use the said game of Shuffle-board in any such house , nor in any other house used as common for such purpose , upon payn for every Keeper of such house to forfeit for every such offence twenty shillings : and for every person playing at the said game in any such house , to forfeit for everie such offence five shillings : Nor shall any person at any time play or game for any monie , or mony-worth upon penalty of forfeiting treble the value therof : one half to the partie in-forming , the other half to the Treasurie . And any Magistrate may hear and deter-min any offence against this Law . [1646 1647]

*penalties.*

*No gaming for mony on pen: of treble value.*

## Generall Court.

IT is ordered , and by this Court declared that the Governour and Deputie Gover-nour joyntly consenting , or any three Assistants concurring in consent shall have power out of Court to reprive a condemned malefactor till the next Court of Assistants: or Generall Court . And that the General Court only shall have power to pardon a condemned malefactor .

*Who have power to Re-prive.*

*to pardon.*

Also it is declared that the General Court hath libertie and Authoritie to send forth any member of this Common-wealth , of what qualitie and condition or office whatso-ever into forrein parts , about any publick Message or negociation : notwithstanding any office or relation whatsoever . Provided the partie so sent be acquainted with the affairs he goeth about, and be willing to undertake the service .

*None free frō forrein Am-baſſie, that accepts the service.*

Nor shall any General Court be diſſolved or adjourned without the consent of the major part therof. [1641] *See Counsell, Courts.*

*Major part in Gen: Court diſſolve or adjourn.*

## Governour.

IT is ordered , and by this Court declared that the Governour shall have a casting vote whensoever an *equivote* shall fall out in the Court of Assistants , or general Assemblie: so shall the President or Moderatour have in all civil Courts or Assemblies [1641] *See Gen: Court.*

*A casting vote in the Gover: and Preſid: in Courts &c.*

## Heresie.

ALTHOUGH *no humane power be Lord over the Faith & Consciences of men , and therfore may not conſtrein them to beleive or profeſſe against their Consciences : yet becauſe ſuch as bring in damnable hereſies, tending to the ſubverſion of the Christian Faith, and destruction of the ſoules of men, ought duly to be reſtreined from ſuch notorious im-piety , it is therfore ordered and decreed by this Court ;*

That if any Christian within this Jurisdiction shall go about to subvert and de-stroy the christian Faith and Religion , by broaching or mainteining any damnable hereſie ; as denying the immortalitie of the Soul , or the resurrection of the body , or any sin to be repented of in the Regenerate , or any evil done by the outward man to be accounted sin : or denying that Christ gave himself a Ransom for our sins , or shal affirm that wee are not justified by his Death and Righteousnes , but by the perfection of our own works ; or shall deny the moralitie of the fourth commandement , or shall indeavour to seduce others to any the heriſies aforementioned , everie such person con-tinuing obstinate therin after due means of conviction shall be sentenced to Baniſh-ment . [1646]

*Baniſhment.*

## Hydes & Skins.

WHERAS *some persons more ſeeking their own private advantage then the good of the publick doe transport raw hydes & pelts, it is ordered and by this Court enacted,* That henceforth no person shall deliver aboard any ship or other veſſell , direct-ly or indirectly any raw hyde , skin, pelt or leather unwrought with intent to have the same

*Raw hides.*

same transported out of this Jurisdiction upon pain to forfeit the same or the value therof . And that no Master of any ship or vessel shall receive any raw hyde , skin, pelt , or leather unwrought directly or indirectly, aboard his ship or vessel to be so transported upon the like penalty . Provided that any person stranger or other may transport any hydes or skins brought hither from beyond the seas by way of Merchandize , or the skins of Beaver, Moos, Bear and Otter . [1646]

### Hygh-wayes.

*To the end there may be convenient high-wayes for Travellers , it is ordered by the Authoritie of this Court ;*

That all common high-wayes shall be such as may be most easie, and safe for travellers : to which purpose everie town (where any such high-way is made, or to be made) shall appoint two or three men of the next town, whose Inhabitants have most occasion therof, chosen & appointed by their said town, who shal from time to time lay out all common high-wayes where they may be most convenient ; notwithstanding any mans proprietie, (so as it occasion not the pulling down of any mans house , or laying open any garden or orchard): who in common grounds or where the soyle is wet, myrie , or verie rockie shall lay out such high-wayes the wyder , *viz:* six, eight, ten or more rods .

*By whom layd out.*

*Places exempted:*

Provided that if any man be therby damaged in his improved ground the town shall make him reasonable satisfaction by estimation of those of the two towns that layd out the same . And if such persons deputed cannot agree in either case it shall be referred to the County Court of that Shire ; or to the Court of Assistants who shall have power to hear and determin the Case . And if any person finde himselfe justly grieved with any act or thing done by the persons deputed aforesaid : he may appeal to the County Court aforesaid , or to the Court of Assistants , but if he be found to complain without cause he shall surely pay all charges of the parties and Court during that Action and also be fined to the Countrie as the Court shall adjudge . [1639]

*Recompence to Propriet:*

*Appeal.*

2 It is ordered and declared by this Court that the selected Towns-men of everie town have power to lay out (by themselves or others) particular and private wayes concerning their own town only : so as no damage be done to any man without due recompence to be given by the judgement of the said Towns-men , and one or two chosen by the said Towns-men and one or two chosen by the partie : and if any man shall finde himselfe justly greived he may appeal to the next County Court of that Shire who shall doe justice therin on both hands as in other cases of appeals . [1642]

*Private wayes in towns.*

3 *UPON information that divers high-wayes are much annoyed and incumbred by gates and rayls erected upon them , it is ordered and enacted by the Authoritie of this Court ,*

That upon any information or complaint made either to the court of Assistants, or any County Court or to any Magistrate of any such gates or rayls erected, or to be erected upon any common high-way , the same Court or Magistrate shall appoint a Committee of discreet and indifferent men to view such incumbrance, and to order the reformation therof . And if the parties whom it shall concern shall not submit to such orders , they shall require them to appear at the next Court for that Shire : and also shall certifie the incumbrance found and order by them made , under their hands unto the said Court , or appear in person to prosecute the cause; where it shall be heard and determined for the ease and conveniencie of Travellers , with due respect to the Proprietors cost and damage , but no person shal stand charged with the repair of common high-wayes through his own ground . [1647]

*One Magistr: power to order redresse*

### Idlenes.

*It* is ordered by this Court and Authoritie therof , that no person , Housholder or other shall spend his time idlely or unprofitably under pain of such punishment as the Court of Assistants or County Court shall think meet to inflict . And for

this

**Constabl's care and dutie**

**The power of two Assistants**

this end it is ordered that the Constable of everie place shall use speciall care and diligence to take knowledge of offenders in this kinde , especially of common coasters, unprofitable fowlers and tobacco takers , and present the same unto the two next Assistants , who shall have power to hear and determin the cause , or transfer it to the next Court . [1633]

### Jesuits.

THIS Court taking into consideration the great wars, combustions and divisions which are this day in *Europe* : and that the same are observed to be raysed and fomented chiefly by the secret underminings , and solicitations of those of the *Jesuiticall Order*, men brought up and devoted to the religion and court of *Rome* ; which hath occasioned divers States to expell them their territories ; for prevention wherof among our selves , It is ordered and enacted by Authoritie of this Court ,

**One Magistr:**

**Banishment.**

That no Jesuit, or spiritual or ecclesiastical person [as they are termed] ordained by the authoritie of the Pope, or Sea of Rome shall henceforth at any time repair to , or come within this Jurisdiction :    And if any person shal give just cause of suspicion that he is one of such Societie or Order he shall be brought before some of the Magistrates, and if he cannot free himselfe of such suspicion he shall be committed to prison , or bound over to the next Court of Assistants , to be tryed and proceeded with by Banishment or otherwise as the Court shall see cause :    and if any person so banished shall be taken the second time within this Jurisdiction upon lawfull tryall and conviction he shall be put to death .    Provided this Law shall not extend to any such Jesuit, spiritual or ecclesiasticall person as shall be cast upon our shoars, by ship-wrack or other accident , so as he continue no longer then till he may have opportunitie of passage for his departure ; nor to any such as shall come in company with any Messenger hither upō publick occasions , or any Merchant or Master of any ship, belonging to any place not in emmitie with the State of *England,* or our selves , so as they depart again with the same Messenger , Master or Merchant , and behave themselves in-offensively during their aboad heer . [1647]

### Impost.

**Worronoco.**

IT is ordered by Authoritie of this Court that *Worronoco* upon *Conecticot* lying within this Jurisdiction shall be , and be reputed as a part of the town of *Springfield* and lyable to all charges there , as other parts of the same town , until upon erecting some other Plantation neer unto it it shall be thought fit by this Court to annex it to such new Plantation .

**Trading-houses.**

It is also ordered that the Trading-house at *Worronoco* and all other Trading-houses erected or to be erected , mainteined or used within this Jurisdiction , for trading with the Indians only or chiefly shall be contributarie to all publick and common charges, both in Town and Countrie , and everie such person as shall inhabit or trade in any such Trading-house or neer the same shall pay unto the publick Treasurie ( by the hands

**Two pence a skin.**

of such as shall be assigned to receive the same) for everie skin of Beaver, Otter, Bear or Moose two pence .    And if such person so assigned shall have cause to suspect that any such Trader hath not given a true account of all such skins so traded , he shall inform one of the next Magistrates therof , who shall send for such Trader and require him to deliver account upon his oath , which if he shall refuse to doe , he may commit him to prison or take *Bond* with Suretie for his appearance at the next Court of Assistants to answer his contempt , and be proceeded with according to justice .

**Forfeit.**

And it is farther ordered that all such skins so received , by way of trading , in, or neer any such Trading-house for which the said *Impost* of two pence a skin shall not be satisfied within one week after demaund therof shall be forfeited to the publick Treasurie , or the value therof ;    to be levied by *Warrant* from any one Magistrate upon any skins or other goods in such Trading-house . [1647]

2 *For*

2 *For the better support of the Government of this Common-wealth and the maintainance of Fortifications for the protecting and safe-guarding of our Coasts and Harbours, for our selves and others that come to trade with us , it is ordered by this Court and the Authoritie therof,*

That every person , Merchant, Seaman, or other that shall bring wines into any our Harbours, in any ships or vessels whatsoever (except they come directly from *England* as their first Port) before they land any of the said wines , more or lesse , shall first make entrie of as many Buts , Pipes , or other vessels, as they or any of them shall put on shore, by a note under their hands, delivered unto the Officer at his house (who is to receive the Customs) upon pain of forfeiture and confiscation of all such wines as are landed before such entrie made, wheresoever found , the one halfe to the Countrie, the other halfe to the Officer : and the Merchants or Owners of such wines of any kinde, as soon as he lands them, shall deliver and pay unto the said Officer , what is due for Custom of them according to this Order, in wine according to the proportion of the goodnes of the parcel that is brought in, as the Officer and Owner can agree, to the contentment and satisfaction of the said Officer , or else the Owner and Officer to nominate a third man who shall put a finall price between them , in point of valuation of the wines for Customs : but if they cannot agree, upon notice from the Officer unto the Treasurer for the time being, he shall determin the price therof, and being so ordered the Officer and Merchant shall accept therof .

And it is farther ordered that he that is the cheife Officer to receive such Customes shall have under him a Deputie or Deputies who shall be as Searchers or waytors in severall places to take up such wines, by the cheif Officers appointment , and to take notice of what is landed in any place that the Country be not defrauded, who shall have such due recompence as the cheif Officer in his discretion shall agree with them for, either by the Butt or Pipe or by the year . All wines to pay customs according to these rates following *viz:* for every Butt or pipe of *Fyall* wines or any other wines of those Western Islands five shillings . For everie Pipe of *Madarie* wines six shillings eight pence . For everie Butt or Pipe of *Sherris* sack, *Malego* or *Canarie* wines ten shillings . For *Muscadels, Malmsies* and other wines from the *Streights* ten shillings . For Bastards, Tents & Alligants ten shillings : and proportionably for greater or lesser vessels of each kinde. For everie Hogshead of French wines two shillings six pence , and proportionably for greater or lesser vessels .

*And for better recovering of any such Customs of wines or forfeitures , for not entering according to this Order and for refusing of payment of such Customs to the satisfaction of the Officer , it is further ordered,*

That the said Officer hath heerby power and is required to goe into all Houses or Cellars where he knoweth or suspecteth any wine to be , and from time to time shall seiz upon such wines as are not entred according to this Order : and also seiz upon, and take possession of so much wines as to make payment of what Custom is due according to entries made , and is refused or neglected to be paid in due manner according to this Order . And all Constables and other Officers are heerby required to assist and ayd the Officer in the discharge of his duty , and helping to break open such Houses or Cellars, if the Owners of such wines shal refuse to open their doors or deliver their keys in a peacable way . And any Smith, Carter, Owner of boat, Porter or other that shall be required by the Officer to put to their hand to help and assist in taking, loading & transporting such wines for the use of the Country, and shall refuse or neglect such service for due hire shall forfeit to the common Treasurie ten shillings for everie such default, to be levied by the Constable by *warrant* from any one Magistrate . And all debts due unto the Countrie for custom of wines , where wines are not to be found, they are to be recovered by way of Action , according to a course of law as in other cases , and this Order to be in force to recover Customs from all those that have landed wine in this Jurisdiction already and not payd Custom .

## Impreſſes.

IT is ordered, and by this Court declared, that no man ſhall be compelled to any publick work, or ſervice, unleſſe the Preſſe be grounded upon ſome act of the General Court; and have reaſonable allowance therfore: nor ſhall any man be compelled in perſon to any office, work, wars, or other publick ſervice that is neceſſarly and ſufficiently exempted, by any natural or perſonal impediment; as by want of years, greatnes of age, defect of minde, failing of ſenſes, or impotencye of lims. Nor ſhall any man be compelled to go out of this Juriſdiction upon any offenſive wars, which this Common-wealth, or any of our freinds or confœderates ſhall voluntarily undertake; but only upõ ſuch vindictive and defenſive wars, in our own behalf, or the behalf of our freinds and confœderates; as ſhall be enterprized by the counſell, and conſent of a General Court, or by Authoritie derived from the ſame. Nor ſhall any mans cattle or goods of what kinde ſoever be preſſed, or taken for any publick uſe or ſervice; unles it be by *Warrant* grounded upon ſome act of the General Court: nor without ſuch reaſonable prizes and hire as the ordinarie rates of the Countrie doe afford. And if his cattle or goods ſhall periſh, or ſuffer damage in ſuch ſervice, the Owner ſhall be ſufficiently recompenced. [1641]

## Impriſonment.

IT is ordered, and by this Court declared; that no mans perſon ſhall be reſtreined or impriſoned by any authoritie whatſoever before the Law hath ſentenced him therto: if he can put in ſufficent ſecuritie, *Bayle* or *Mainprize* for his appearance, and good behaviour in the mean time: unles it be in crimes Capital, and contempt in open Court, and in ſuch caſes where ſome expreſſe Act of Court doth allow it. [1641]

## Indians.

IT is ordered by Authoritie of this Court; that no perſon whatſoever ſhall henceforth buy land of any Indian, without licence firſt had & obtained of the General Court: and if any ſhall offend heerin, ſuch land ſo bought ſhall be forfeited to the Countrie.

Nor ſhall any man within this Juriſdiction directly or indirectly amend, repair, or cauſe to be amended or repaired any gun, ſmall or great, belonging to any Indian, nor ſhall indeavour the ſame. Nor ſhall ſell or give to any Indian, directly or indirectly anyſuch gun, or any gun-powder, ſhot or lead, or ſhot-mould, or any militarie weapons or armour: upon payn of ten pounds fine, at the leaſt for everie ſuch offence: and that the court of Aſſiſtants ſhall have power to increaſe the Fine; or to impoſe corporall puniſhment (where a Fine cannot be had) at their diſcretion.

It is alſo ordered by the Authoritie aforeſaid that everie town ſhall have power to reſtrein all Indians from profaning the Lords day. [1633 1637 1641]

2 *Wheras it appeareth to this Court that notwithſtanding the former Laws, made againſt ſelling of guns, powder and Amunition to the Indians, they are yet ſupplyed by indirect means, it is therfore ordered by this Court and Authoritie therof;*

That if any perſon after publication heerof, ſhall ſell, give or barter any gun or guns, powder, bullets, ſhot or lead to any Indian whatſoever, or unto any perſon inhabiting out of this Juriſdiction without licence of this Court, or the court of Aſſiſtants, or ſome two Magiſtrates, he ſhall forfeit for everie gun ſo ſold, given or bartered ten pounds: and for everie pound of powder five pounds: and for everie pound of bullets, ſhot or lead fourty ſhillings: and ſo proportionably for any greater or leſſer quantitie. [1642]

3 It is ordered by this Court and Authoritie therof, that in all places, the Engliſh and ſuch others as co-inhabit within our Juriſdiction ſhall keep their cattle frõ deſtroying the Indians corn, in any ground where they have right to plant; and if any of their corn be deſtroyed for want of fencing, or hearding; the town ſhall make ſatisfaction, and ſhall have power among themſelves to lay the charge where the occaſion of the damage did ariſe. Provided that the Indians ſhall make proof that the cattle of ſuch a town, farm, or perſon did the damage. And for encouragement of

---

Margin notes:

Only by Gen Court upõ due recompence.

Preſ-free, for defects:

from forrein warrs:

Limitation.

for cattle and goods.
Limitation twofold,

Recompence

Who be baylable.

Licence to buy their land.

none muſt repair their guns

nor ſell gun or amunition on pen: of 10 li.

Who may reſtrein them frõ profaning the Sabbath.

No arms ſold to Indian or Forreiner without licence.

on forſ: for a gun 10 li, for 1 li. powder 5 li. 1 li. ſhot &c: 40 ſs.

preſervation of their corn.

of the Indians toward the fencing in of their corn fields, such towns, farms or persons, whose cattle may annoy them that way, shall direct, assist and help them in felling of trees, ryving, and sharpening of rayls, & holing of posts : allowing one English-man to three or more Indians . And shall also draw the fencing into place for them, and allow one man a day or two toward the setting up the same, and either lend or sell them tools to finish it . Provided that such Indians, to whom the Countrie, or any town hath given, or shall give ground to plant upon, or that shall purchase ground of the English shall fence such their corn fields or ground at their own charge as the English doe or should doe ; and if any Indians refuse to fence their corn ground (being tendred help as aforesaid) in the presence and hearing of any Magistrate or selected Townsmen being met together they shall keep off all cattle or lose one half of their damages .

And it is also ordered that if any harm be done at any time by the Indians unto the English in their cattle; the Governour or Deputie Governour with two of the Assistants of any three Magistrates or any County Court may order satisfaction according to law and justice . [1640 1648]

4 *Considering that one end in planting these parts was to propagate the true Religion unto the Indians : and that divers of them are become subjects to the English and have ingaged themselves to be willing and ready to understand the Law of God , it is therfore ordered and decreed ,*

That such necessary and wholsom Laws, which are in force, and may be made from time to time , to reduce them to civilitie of life shall be once in the year (if the times be safe) made known to them, by such fit persons as the General Court shall nominate , having the help of some able Interpreter with them .

*Considering also that interpretation of tongues is appointed of God for propagating the Truth : and may therfore have a blessed successe in the hearts of others in due season , it is therfore farther ordered and decreed ,*

That two Ministers shall be chosen by the Elders of the Churches everie year at the Court of Election , and so be sent with the consent of their Churches ( with whomsoever will freely offer themselves to accompany them in that service) to make known the heavenly counsell of God among the Indians in most familiar manner , by the help of some able Interpreter ; as may be most available to bring them unto the knowledge of the truth , and their conversation to the Rules of Jesus Christ . And for that end that somthing be allowed them by the General Court, to give away freely unto those Indians whom they shall perceive most willing & ready to be instructed by them.

And it is farther ordered and decreed by this Court ; that no Indian shall at any time *powaw* , or performe outward worship to their false gods : or to the devil in any part of our Jurisdiction ; whether they be such as shall dwell heer , or shall come hither : and if any shall transgresse this Law, the *Powawer* shall pay five pounds ; the Procurer five pounds ; and every other countenancing by his presence or otherwise being of age of discretion twenty shillings . [1646]

### Inditements .

IF any person shall be indicted of any capital crime (who is not then in *durance*) & shall refuse to render his person to some Magistrate within one month after three Proclaimations publickly made in the town where he usually abides , there being a month betwixt Proclaimation and Proclaimation , his lands and goods shall be seized to the use of the common Treasurie, till he make his lawfull appearance . And such withdrawing of himselfe shall stand in stead of one wittnes to prove his crime , unles he can make it appear to the Court that he was necessarily hindred . [1646]

### In-keepers, Tippling, Drunkenes.

FORASMUCH *as there is a necessary use of houses of common entertainment in every Common-wealth , and of such as retail wine, beer and victuals ; yet because there are so many abuses of that lawfull libertie , both by persons entertaining and persons entertained , there is also need of strict Laws and Rules to regulate such an employment : It is therfore ordered by this Court and Authoritie therof ;*

E That

**No common Victuailer. Cook ,Vintner &c without licence.**

**On pen: 5 li.**

**Signe**

**No beer above two pence the quart Any may sel out of doors of 1 d. a quart,**

**In-holders forfeit**

**Penalty of drüknes 10 s. exc: 3 s. 4 d. Tipl: unsaſonably.**

**Stocks.**

**Proviso,**

**The laws further extent**

**Seecōd offence double penal: Third offen: Whipping,**

**Stocks,**

**Fourth offen:**

**Victuailer cōviết a third time diſabl d:**

That no perſon or perſons ſhall at any time under any pretence or colour whatſoever undertake to be a common Victuailer, Keeper of a Cooks ſhop, or houſe for common entertainment, Taverner, or publick ſeller of wine, ale, beer or ſtrong-water (by re-tale), nor ſhall any ſell wine privatly in his houſe or out of doors by a leſſe quantitie, or under a quarter cask: without approbation of the ſelected Townſ-men and Licence of the Shire Court where they dwell: upon pain of forfeiture of five pounds for everie ſuch offence, or impriſonment at pleaſure of the Court, where ſatis-faction cannot be had.

And every perſon ſo licenced for common entertainment ſhall have ſome inoffen-ſive Signe obvious for ſtrangers direction, and ſuch as have no ſuch Signe after three months ſo licenced from time to time ſhall loſe their licence: and others allowed in their ſtead. And any licenced perſon that ſelleth beer ſhall not ſell any above two-pence the ale-quart: upon penaltie of three ſhillings four pence for everie ſuch offence. And it is permitted to any that will to ſell beer out of doors at a pennie the ale-quart and under.

Neither ſhall any ſuch licenced perſon aforeſaid ſuffer any to be drunken, or drink exceſſively viz: above half a pinte of wine for one perſon at one time; or to con-tinue tippling above the ſpace of half an hour, or at unſeaſonable times, or after nine of the clock at night in, or about any of their houſes on penaltie of five ſhillings for everie ſuch offence.

And everie perſon found drunken viz: ſo that he be therby bereaved or diſabled in the uſe of his underſtanding, appearing in his ſpeech or geſture in any the ſaid houſ-es or elſewhere ſhall forfeit ten ſhillings. And for exceſſive drinking three ſhillings four pence. And for continuing above half an hour tippling two ſhillings ſix pence. And for tippling at unſeaſonable times, or after nine a clock at night five ſhillings: for everie offence in theſe particulars being lawfully convict therof. And for want of payment ſuch ſhall be impriſoned untill they pay: or be ſet in the *Stocks* one hour or more [in ſome open place] as the weather will permit not exceeding three hours at one time.

Provided notwithſtanding ſuch licenced perſons may entertain ſea-faring men, or land travellers in the night-ſeaſon, when they come firſt on ſhore, or from their journy for their neceſſarie refreſhment, or when they prepare for their voyage or jour-nie the next day early; ſo there be no diſorder among them; and alſo Strangers, Lodg-ers or other perſons in an orderly way may continue in ſuch houſes of common enter-tainment during meal times, or upon lawfull buſines what time their occaſions ſhall require.

Nor ſhall any Merchant, Cooper, Owner or Keeper of wines or other perſons that have the government of them ſuffer any perſon to drink to exceſſe, or drunkenes, in any their wine-Cellars, Ships, or other veſſels or places where wines doe lye; on pain to forfeit for each perſon ſo doing ten ſhillings.

And if any perſon offend in drunkenes, exceſſive or long drinking the ſecōd time they ſhall pay double Fines. And if they fall into the ſame offence the third time they ſhall pay treble Fines. And if the parties be not able to pay the Fines then he that is found drunk ſhall be puniſhed by whipping to the number of ten ſtripes: and he that offends in exceſſive or long drinking ſhall be put into the ſtocks for three hours when the weather may not hazzard his life or lims. And if they offend the fourth time they ſhall be impriſoned untill they put in two ſufficient Sureties for their good behaviour.

And it is farther ordered that if any perſon that keepeth, or heerafter ſhall keep a common houſe of entertainmen, ſhall be lawfully convicted the third time for any offence againſt this Law: he ſhall (for the ſpace of three years next enſuing the ſaid conviction) be diſabled to keep any ſuch houſe of entertainment, or ſell wine, beer or the like; unles the Court aforeſaid ſhall ſee cauſe to continue them.

It is farther ordered that everie In-keeper, or Victuailer ſhall provide for the
entertainment

of strangers horses *viz*: one or more inclosures for Summer and hay and provender for Winter with convenient stable room and attendance, under penaltie of two shillings six pence for everie dayes default, and double damage to the partie therby wronged (except it be by inevitable accident.

And it is farther ordered by the Authoritie aforesaid, that no Taverner or seller of wine by retale, licenced as aforesaid shall take above nine pounds profit by the Butt or Pipe of wine, (and proportionably for all other vessels) toward his wast in drawing and otherwise: out of which allowance everie such Taverner or Vintner shall pay fifty shillings by the Butt or Pipe and proportionably for all other vessels to the Countrie. For which he shall account with the Auditor general or his Deputie every six months and discharge the same. All which they may doe by selling six pence a quart in retale (which they shall no time exceed) more then it cost by the Butt, beside the benefit of their art and mysterie which they know how to make use of. And everie Taverner or Vintner shall give a true account and notice unto the Auditor or his Deputie of everie vessell of wine he buies from time to time within three dayes; upon pain of forfeiting the same or the value therof.

And all such as retale strong waters shall pay in like manner two pence upon everie quart to the use of the Country, who also shall give notice to the Auditor or his Deputie of everie case and bottle or other quantitie they buy within three dayes upon payn of forfeiture as before.

Also it is ordered that in all places where week-day Lectures are kept, all Taverners, Victuailers and Tablers that are within a mile of the Meeting-house, shall from time to time clear their houses of all persons able to goe to the Meeting, during the time of the exercise (except upon extraordinary cause, for the necessarie refreshing of strangers unexpectedly repairing to them) upon pain of five shillings for every such offence over and besides the penalties incurred by this Law for any other disorder.

It is also ordered that all offences against this Law may be heard and determined by any one Magistrate, who shall heerby have power by *Warrant* to send for parties, and witnesses, and to examin the said witnesses upon oath and the parties without oath, concerning any of these offences: and upon due conviction either by view of the said Magistrate, or affirmation of the Constable, and one sufficient witnes with circumstances concurring, or two witnesses, or confession of the partie to levie the said severall fines, by *Warrant* to the Constable for that end, who shall be accountable to the Auditor for the same.

And if any person shall voluntarily confesse his offence against this Law in any the particulars therof, his oath shall be taken in evidence and stand good against any other offending at the same time.

Lastly, it is ordered by the Authoritie aforesaid that all Constables may, and shall from time to time duly make search throughout the limits of their towns upon Lords dayes, and Lecture dayes in times of Exercise; and also at all other times, so oft as they shall see cause for all offences and offenders against this Law in any the particulars therof. And if upon due information, or complaint of any of their Inhabitants, or other credible persons whether Taverner, Victuailer, Tabler or other; they shall refuse or neglect to make search as aforesaid, or shall not to their power perform all other things belonging to their place and Office of Constableship: then upon complaint and due proof before any one Magistrate within three months after such refusall or neglect; they shall be fined for everie such offence ten shillings, to be levied by the Marshal as in other cases by *Warrant* from such Magistrate before whom they are convicted, or *Warrant* from the Treasurer upon notice from such Magistrate. [1645 1646 1647] See *Gaming, Licences.*

## Juries, Jurors.

I T is ordered by this Court and Authoritie therof, that the Constable of everie town upon *Proces* from the Recorder of each Court, shall give timely notice to the Freemen of their town, to choose so many able discreet men as the *Proces* shall direct which

E 2

Proviso for horses.

Vintner.

pay 50 s. § Butt to the Countrie.

Juries to give account.

Two pence a quart for retail of strong water.

Com: houses cleared in Lecture time.

One Magistr: may hear &c.

Fines levied.

Delinquents testimonie.

Const: search

Constables neglect.

which men so chosen he shall warn to attend the Court whereto they are appointed, and shall make return of the *Proces* unto the Recorder aforesaid : which men so chosen shall be *impannelled* and sworn truly to try betwixt partie and partie, who shall finde the matter of fact with the damages and costs according to their evidence, and the Judges shall declare the Sentence (or direct the Jurie to finde) according to the law. And if there be any matter of apparent equitie as upon the forfeiture of an Obligation, breach of covenant without damage, or the like, the Bench shall determin such matter of equitie.

2 Nor shall any tryall passe upon any for life or bannishment but by a special Jurie so summoned for that purpose, or by the General Court.

3 It is also ordered by the Authoritie aforesaid that there shall be Grand-Juries summoned everie year unto the several Courts, in each Jurisdiction ; to inform the Court of any misdemeanours that they shall know or hear to be committed by any person or persons whatsoever within this Jurisdiction. And to doe any other service of the Common-wealth that according to law they shall be injoyned to by the said Court; and in all cases wherin evidence is so obscure or defective that the Jurie cannot clearly and safely give a positive verdict, whether it be Grand, or Petty Jurie, it shall have libertie to give a *Non liquet* or a special verdict, in which last, that is, a special verdict the judgement of the Cause shall be left unto the Bench. And all Jurors shall have libertie in matters of fact if they cannot finde the *main issue* yet to finde and present in their verdict so much as they can.

4 And if the Bench and Jurors shall so differ at any time about their verdict that either of them cannot proceed with peace of conscience, the Case shall be referred to the General Court who shall take the question from both and determin it.

5 And it is farther ordered that whensoever any Jurie of tryalls, or Jurors are not clear in their judgements or consciences, concerning any Case wherin they are to give their verdict, they shall have libertie, in open Court to advise with any man they shall think fit to resolve or direct them, before they give in their verdict. And no Freeman shall be compelled to serve upon Juries above one ordinary Court in a year : except Grand-jurie men, who shall hold two Courts together at the least, and such others as shall be summoned to serve in case of life and death or bannishment. [1634] [1641 1642] *See Secresie.*

## Iustice.

IT is ordered, and by this Court declared; that every person within this Jurisdiction, whether Inhabitant or other shall enjoy the same justice and law that is general for this Jurisdiction which wee constitute and execute one towards another, in all cases proper to our cognisance without partialitie or delay. [1641]

### Lands, Free lands,

IT is ordered, and by this Court declared ; that all our Lands and Heritages shall be free from all *Fines* and *Licences* upon alienations, and from all *Hariots, Wardships, Liveries, Primerseizins,* year, day and wast, *Escheats* and forfeitures, upon the death of Parents or Ancesters, be they natural, unnatural, casual or judicial and that for ever. [1641] *See Abilitie, Escheats, Strangers.*

### Leather.

THIS Court taking into serious consideration the several deceits and abuses which in other places have been and are commonly practiced by the Tanners, Curriers and workers of leather, as also the abuses and inconveniences which acrue to the severall members of this Common-wealth, by leather not sufficiently tanned and wrought, which is occasioned by the negligence and unskilfulnes of those severall trades-men which before, in, & after it is in the hands of the Tanner may be much bettered or impaired, for prevention whereof, it is ordered by this Court and the Authoritie therof;

That no person using or occupying the feat or mysterie of a Butcher, Currier, or
shoe-maker

---

*Side notes (left margin):*

Juries for tryals.

Verdict according to fact

Equitie and law in the same case

Tryall for life &c: by 12 men

Juries for inquirie

may be for tryal also,

Positive verd: Non liquet

Partial verd:

Differ: twixt Jury & Bench issued

Jurie in their doubts may advise openly none serv but once a year except:

Forreiners libertie.

Shoe-maker by himfelfe or any other , fhall ufe or exercife the feat or myfterie of a Tanner on pain of forfeiture of fix fhillings eight pence for everie hyde or skin by him or them fo tanned whileft he or they fhall ufe or occupie any of the myfteries aforefaid .

Nor fhall any Tanner during his ufing the faid trade of tanning , ufe or occupie the feat or myfterie of either Butcher , Currier or Shoo-maker by himfelf or any other upon pain of the like forfeiture .

Nor fhall any Butcher by himfelf or any other perfon gafh or cut any hyde of ox , bull , fteer , or cow in fleaing therof , or otherwife wherby the fame fhall be impaired or hurt , on pain of forfeiture for everie fuch gafh or cut in any hyde or skin twelve pence .

Nor fhall any perfon or perfons henceforth bargain , buy , make any contract , or befpeak any rough hyde of ox , bull , fteer or cow in the hair , but only fuch perfons as have and doe ufe and exercife the art of tanning .

Nor fhall any perfon or perfons ufing , or which fhall ufe the myfterie or facultie of tanning at any time or times heerafter , offer or put to fale any kinde of leather , which fhall be infufficiently or not throughly tanned , or which fhall not then have been after the tanning therof well and throughly dryed , upon pain of forfeiting fo much of his or their faid leather as by any Searcher or Sealer of leather lawfully ap-pointed fhall be found infufficiently tanned , or not throughly dryed as aforefaid.

Nor fhall any perfon or perfons ufing or occupying the myfterie of tanning , fet any their Fats in tan-hills or other places , where the woozes or leather put to tan in the fame fhall or may take any unkinde heats ; nor fhall put any leather into any hot or warm woozes whatfoever on pain of twenty pounds for everie fuch offence .

Nor fhall any perfon or perfons ufing or occupying the myfterie or facultie of currying , currie any kinde of leather , except it be well and throughly tanned ; nor fhall currie any hyde being not throughly dryed after his wet feafon ; in which wet feafon he fhall not ufe any ftale , urin , or any other deceitfull or fubtil mixture , thing , way or means to corrupt or hurt the fame : nor fhall currie any leather meet for utter fole leather with any other then good hard tallow , nor with any leffe of that then the leather will receive : nor fhall currie any kinde of leather meet for upper leather and inner foles , but with good and fufficient ftuffe , being frefh and not falt , and throughly liquored till it will receive no more : nor fhall burn or fcald any hyde or leather in the currying , but fhall work the fame fufficiently in all points and refpects; on pain of forfeiture for everie fuch offence or act done contrary to the true meaning of this Order the full value of everie fuch hyde marred by his evil workmanfhip or handling , which fhall be judged by two , or more fufficient and honeft skilfull perfons , Curriers or others , on their oath given to them for that end by any Affiftant .

And everie town where need is , or fhall be , fhall choofe one or two perfons of the moft honeft and skilfull within their feveral Townfhips , and prefent them unto the County Court , or one Magiftrate who fhall appoint and fwear the faid perfons : by their difcretion to make fearch and view within the Precincts of their limits as oft as they fhall think good and need fhall be , who fhall have a Mark or Seal prepared by each town for that purpofe , and the faid Searchers or one of them fhall keep the fame , and therewith fhall feal fuch leather as they fhall finde fufficient in all points and no other .

And if the faid Searchers , or any of them fhall finde any leather fold , or offered to be fold , brought , or offered to be fearched or fealed , which fhall be tanned , wrought , converted or ufed contrary to the true intent and meaning of this Order , it fhall be lawfull for the faid Searchers , or any of them to feiz all fuch leather and to retain the fame in their cuftodie , untill fuch time as it be tryed by fuch Tryers ,

E 3 and

| | |
|---|---|
| Butcher Currier Shoom. no Tanner. | |
| Tanner no Butcher, Currier Shoom. | |
| Gafh:hyde or skin 12 d | |
| Rough hyds | |
| well taññed & dryed. Penaltie. | |
| Leather taking ükinde heats. Penaltie 20 li | |
| Curriers duty | |
| Penaltie. | |
| Searchers fworn. their dutie | |
| to feale. | |
| feiz defective | |

and in such manner as in this Order is appointed viz. upon the forfeiture of any leather the Officer so seizing the same, shall within three dayes call to him four or six men, honest, and skilfull in such ware to view the same in the presence of the partie (who shall have timely notice therof) or without him, who shall certifie upon their oaths unto the next County Court for that Shire, or unto one of the Assistants the defect of the same leather, except the partie shall before submit to their judgement.

The like power shall the said Searcher have to search all leather wrought into shoos and boots, as also to seize all such as they finde to be made of insufficient leather, or not well and sufficiently wrought up. And if any Searcher or Sealer of leather shall refuse with convenient-speed to seal any leather sufficiently tanned, wrought and used according to the true meaning of this Order, or shall seal that which shall be insufficient, then everie such Searcher and Sealer of leather shall forseit for everie such offence the full value of so much as shall be insufficiently tanned.

And the Fees for searching and sealing of leather shall be one pennie a hyde for any parcel lesse then five, and for all other parcels after the rate of six pence a *Deker*; which the Tanner shall pay upon the sealing of the said leather from time to time.

Lastly, it is ordered by the Authoritie aforesaid that the severall Fines and Forfeitures in this Order mentioned, shall be equally divided into three parts and distributed as followeth v.z. one part to the common Treasurie of the Shire wherin the offence is committed, another third part to the common Treasurie of the Township where such offender inhabiteth, and the other third part to the Seizer or Seizers of such leather, shoos or boots, as is insufficiently tanned, curried or wrought from time to time. [1642]

## Levies.

FORASMUCH as the *Marshals* and other Officers have complained to this Court that they are oftentimes in great doubt how to demean themselves in the execution of their offices, it is ordered by the Authoritie of this Court;

That in case of Fines and Assessements to be levied, and upon Execution in civil Actions, the Officer shall demand the same of the partie, or at his house or place of usuall abode, and upon refusall or non-payment he shall have power (calling the Constable if he see cause for his assistance) to break open the door of any house, chest, or place where he shall have notice that any goods lyable to such Levie or Execution shall be; and if he be to take the person he may doe the like, if upon demand he shall refuse to render himself.

And whatever charges the Officer shall necessarily be put unto upon any such occasion, he shall have power to levie the same, as he doth the debt, Fine, or Execution: and where the Officer shall levie any such goods upon execution as cannot be conveyed to the place where the partie dwells, for whom such Execution shall be levied, without considerable charge, he shall levie the said charge also with the Execution.

The like order shall be observed in levying of Fines. Provided it shall not be lawfull for such Officer to levie any mans necessarie bedding, apparel, tools, or Arms, neither implements of houshold which are for the necessarie upholding of his life, but in such cases he shall levie his land or person according to law: and in no case shall the Officer be put to seek out any mans estate farther then his place of abode; but if the partie will not discover his goods or lands, the Officer may take his person.

And it is also ordered and declared that if any Officer shall doe injurie to any by colour of his Office, in these or any other cases he shall be lyable upon complaint of the partie wronged, by Action or Information to make full restitution. [1647]

## Liberties Common

IT is ordered by this Court , decreed and declared ;  that everie man whether Inhabitant or Forreiner , Free or not Free shall have libertie to come to any pub-lick Court , Counsell , or Town-meeting ;  and either by speech or writing , to move any lawfull , seasonable , or material question ;  or to present any necessarie motion, complaint, petition, bill or information wherof that Meeting hath proper cognisance, so it be done in convenient time, due order and respective manner . [1641]

2  Everie Inhabitant who is an houf-holder shall have free fishing and fowling, in any great Ponds, Bayes, Coves and Rivers so far as the Sea ebs and flows , within the precincts of the town where they dwell , unles the Free-men of the same town , or the General Court have otherwise appropriated them .  Provided that no town shall appropriate to any particular person or persons , any great Pond conteining more then ten acres of land :   and that no man shall come upon anothers proprietie without their leave otherwise then as heerafter expressed ;  the which clearly to determin , it is de-clared that in all creeks, coves and other places, about andupon salt water where the Sea ebs and flows ,  the Proprietor of the land adjoyning shall have proprietie to the low water mark where the Sea doth not ebb above a hundred rods , and not more wheresoever it ebs farther .  Provided that such Proprietor shall not by this libertie have power to stop or hinder the passage of boats or other vessels in , or through any sea creeks, or coves to other mens houses or lands .  And for great Ponds lying in com-mon though within the bounds of some town , it shall be free for any man to fish and fowl there , and may passe and repasse on foot through any mans proprietie for that end, so they trespasse not upon any mans corn or meadow . [1641 1647]

3  Every man of, or within this Jurisdiction shall have free libertie , (notwithstand-ing any civil power ) to remove both himself and his familie at their pleasure out of the same .   Provided there be no legal impediment to the contrary . [1641] See *Arrests, Records, Witnesses.*

## Lying.

WHERAS truth in words as well as in actions is required of all men , especially of Chistians who are the professed Servants of the God of Truth ;   and wheras all lying is contrary to truth , and some sorts of lyes are not only sinfull (as all lyes are) but also pernicious to the Publick-weal , and injurious to particular persons ; it is therfore order-ed by this Court and Authoritie therof ,

That everie person of the age of discretion [which is accounted fourteen years] who shall wittingly and willingly make , or publish any Lye which may be pernicious to the publick weal , or tending to the damage or injurie of any particular person , or with intent to deceive and abuse the people with false news or reports :  and the same duly proved in any Court or before any one Magistrate (who hath heerby power graunted to hear, and determin all offences against this Law) such person shall be fined for the first offence ten shillings , or if the partie be unable to pay the same then to be set in the *stocks* so long as the said Court or Magistrate shall appoint , in some open place, not exceeding two hours .  For the second offence in that kinde wherof any shall be legally convicted the sum of twenty shillings , or be whipped upon the naked body not exceeding ten stripes .  And for the third offence that way fourty shillings, or if the partie be unable to pay , then to be whipped with more stripes, not exceeding fifteen .  And if yet any shall offend in like kinde , and be legally convicted therof, such person, male or female, shall be fined ten shillings a time more then formerly :  or if the partie so offending be unable to pay , then to be whipped with five, or six more stripes then formerly not exceeding fourty at any time .

The aforesaid fines shall be levied, or stripes inflicted either by the Marshal of that Jurisdiction , or Constable of the Town where the offence is committed according

**Marginal notes:**

Freedom in publ. Assemb. [Freemen For no-Frem. [Strangers.

Fishing and fowl: where the Sea ebbs and flows except pro-prieties.

to low water not exceeding 100 rod.

water passag: free & ponds above 10 acrs

Removals free

Age of dif-cretio 14 years

One Magistr. may hear &c: First offence 10 ss or stocks.

Sec: offence 20 shill: or whipped. Third offence 40 shill: or whipped. Fourth offen: 10 ss more or 5 stripes more

Who shall excecute.

according as the Court or Magistrate shall direct .    And such fines so levied shall be paid to the Treasurie of that Shire where the Cause is tried .

And if any person shall finde himselfe greived with the sentence of any such Magistrate out of Court , he may appeal to the next Court of the same Shire , giving sufficient securitie to prosecute his appeal and abide the Order of the Court .    And if the said Court shall judge his appeal causlesse , he shall be double fined and pay the charges of the Court during his Action , or corrected by whipping as aforesaid not exceeding fourtie stripes ; and pay the costs of Court and partie complaining or informing , and of Wittnesses in the Case .

And for all such as being under age of discretion that shall offend in lying contrary to this Order their Parents or Masters shall give them due correction , and that in the presence of some Officer if any Magistrate shall so appoint .    Provided also that no person shall be barred of his just Action of Slaunder , or otherwise by any proceeding upon this Order . [1645]

## *Magiftrates.*

THIS Court being sensible of the great disorder growing in this Common-wealth through the contempts cast upon the civil Authoritie , which willing to prevent , doe order and decree ;

That whosoever shal henceforth openly or willingly defame any Court of justice , or the Sentences or proceedings of the same , or any of the Magistrates or other Judges of any such Court in respect of any Act or Sentence therin passed , and being therof lawfully convict' in any General Court or Court of Assistants shall be punished for the same by Fine, Imprisonment, *Disfranchisement* or Bannishment as the qualitie and measure of the offence shall deserve .

And if any Magistrate or other member of any court shall use any reproachfull , or un-beseeming speeches , or behaviour towards any Magistrate, Judge, or member of the Court in the face of the said Court he shall be sharply reproved , by the Governour, or other principal Judge of the same Court for the time being .    And if the qualitie of the offence be such as shall deserve a farther censure , or if the person so reproved shall reply again without leave , the same Court may proceed to punish any such offender by Fine, or Imprisonment , or it shall be presented to, and censured at the next superiour Court .

2 If in a General Court any miscarriage shall be amongst the Magistrates when they are by themselves , it shall be examined , and sentenced amongst themselves. If amongst the Deputies when they are by themselves , it shall be examined , and sentenced amongst themselves .    If it be when the whole Court is together , it shall be judged by the whole Court , and not severall as before . [1637 1641]

3 And it is ordered by the Authoritie of this Court that the Governour, Deputie Governour , or greater part of the Assistants may upon urgent occasion call a General Court at any time . [1647]

4    *And wheras there may arise some difference of judgement in doubtfull cases , it is therfore farther ordered ;*

That no Law, Order, or Sentence shall passe as an Act of the Court without the consent of the greater part of the Magistrates on the one partie , and the greater number of the Deputies on the other part .

5    *And for preventing all occasions of partial and undue proceeding in Courts of justice , and avoyding of jealousies which may be taken up against Judges in that kinde , it is farther ordered ,*

That in everie Case of civil nature between partie and partie where there shall fall out so neer relation between any Judge and any of the parties as between Father and Son , either by nature or marriage , Brother and Brother ;  in like kinde Uncle and Nephew, Land-lord and Tenent in matters of considerable value , such Judge though he may have libertie to be present in the Court at the time of the tryall , and give reasonable advice in the Case , yet shall have no power to vote or give sentence therin , neither

neither fhall fit as Judge, but beneath the Bench when he fhall fo plead or give advice in the Cafe. [1635] *See Burglary, Caufes, Charges publ: Sect: 3, Death untimely, Drukenes, Elections Sect: 3, Gaming, High-wayes, In-keepers, Leather, Marriage, Mafters Servants, Oaths, Transportation.*

### Man-flaughter.

IT is ordered by this Court and Authoritie therof; that if any perfon in the juft, and neceffarie defence of his life, or the life of any other, fhall kill any perfon attempting to rob, or murther in the field, or high-way, or to break into any dwelling houfe if he conceive he cannot with fafety of his own perfon otherwife take the Felon, or Affailant, or bring him to Tryall he fhall be holden blameles. [1647]

*fe defendendo*

### Marriage.

FOR preventing all unlawfull marriages, it is ordered by this Court and Authoritie therof,

That after due publication heerof no perfons fhall be joyned in marriage before the intention of the parties proceeding therin hath been three times publifhed at fome time of publick Lecture or Town-meeting, in both the towns where the parties or either of them doe ordinarily refide; or be fet up in writing upon fome poft of their Meeting-houfe door in publick view, there to ftand fo as it may eafily be read by the fpace of fourteen dayes. [1639]

Three times publifhed or pofted fourteen dayes

2  *And wheras God hath committed the care and power into the hands of Parents for the difpofing their Children in marriage: fo that it is againft Rule to feek to draw away the affections of young maidens under pretence of purpofe of marriage before their Parents have given way and allowance in that refpect. And wheras it is a common practice in divers places for young men irregularly and diforderly to watch all advantages for their evil purpofes to infinuate into the affections of young maidens, by coming to them in places, and feafons unknown to their Parents, for fuch ends; wherby much evil hath grown amongft us to the difhonour of God and damage of parties, for prevention wherof for time to come it is farther ordered by Authoritie of this Court,*

That whatfoever perfon from henceforth fhall indeavour directly, or indirectly to draw away the affections of any maid in this Jurifdiction under pretence of marriage, before he hath obtained libertie and allowance from her Parents or Governours (or in abfence of fuch) of the neereft Magiftrate; he fhall forfeit for the firft offence five pounds, for the fecond offence toward the fame partie ten pounds, and be bound to forbear any farther attempt and proceedings in that unlawfull defigne without, or againft the allowance aforefaid. And for the third offence upon information, or complaint by fuch Parents or Governours to any Magiftrate, giving *Bond* to profecute the partie, he fhall be committed to prifon, and upon hearing and conviction by the next Court fhall be adjudged to continue in prifon until the Court of Affiftants fhall fee caufe to releafe him. [1647]

No pretence of marriage to any maid without confent of Parents on payn of 5 li firft offence. Sec: offence 10 li: and good behaviour, Third offen: imprifoned.

3  *Wheras divers perfons both men and woemen living within this Jurifdiction whofe Wives, and Husbands are in England, or elf-where, by means wherof they live under great temptations heer, and fome of them committing lewdnes and filthines heer among us, others make love to woemen, and attempt Marriage, and fome have attained it; and fome of them live under fufpicion of uncleannes, and all to the great difhonour of God, reproach of Religion, Common-wealth and Churches, it is therfore ordered by this Court & Authoritie therof (for the prevention of all fuch future evils)*

That all fuch married perfons as aforefaid fhall repair to their faid relations by the firft opportunitie of fhipping upon the pain, or penaltie of twenty pounds, except they can fhew juft caufe to the contrary to the next County Court, or Court of Affiftants to be holden at *Bofton* after they are fummoned by the Conftable there to appear, who are heerby required fo to doe upon pain of twenty fhillings for everie fuch default wittingly made. Provided that this Order doe not extend to fuch as are come over to make way for their families, or are in a tranfient way only for traffick, or merchandize for fome fmall time. [1647]

Mar: perfons to go to their Wives on pain of 20 li. except they fhew caufe. Conftable to Summon on pain of 20 s. Caution.

F                    4 As

4 *As the Ordinance of Marriage is honourable amongst all so should it be accordingly solemnized . It is therfore ordered by this Court and Authoritie therof;*

That no person whatsoever in this Jurisdiction shall joyn any persons together in Marriage but the Magistrate , or such other as the General Court, or Court of Assistants shall authorize in such places where no Magistrate is neer . Nor shall any joyn themselves in Marriage but before some Magistrate , or person authorized as aforesaid. Nor shall any Magistrate , or other person authorized as aforesaid joyn any persons together in Marriage , or suffer them to joyn together in Marriage in their presence before the parties to be married have been published according to Law . [1648] *See Childrens Sect:* 3. 4.

### Marshal.

FORASMUCH *as delay in executing justice is dangerous to any State , and wheras many offenders are punished only by Fines or pecuniarie Mulcts ; if there be delay or neglect in Officers , that such Fines and Penalties are not duly levied , then sin is unpunished , the Name and Ordinance of God may thereby be reproached , it is therfore ordered by this Court and Authoritie therof;*

That everie offender that shall at any time be fined for the breach of any pænal Law , such person or persons so offending shall forthwith pay his or their Fine or Penaltie , or put in securitie speedily to doe it , or else shall be imprisoned , or kept to work till it be payd that no losse may come to the Common-wealth : and what other fines or debts be already due , or shall be due to the Countrie the Marshal for the time being upon *Warrant* from the Treasurer , and according to his oath shall be faithfull in doing the duties of his place , in levying, and returning of the same upon pain of forfeiting two shillings out of his own estate for everie pound , or else such Fine as any Court of justice shall impose on him for his neglect . [1646]    *See Actions, Causes, Clerk of Writs, Oaths.*

### Masters, Servants, Labourers.

IT is ordered by this Court and the Authoritie therof, that no servant, either man or maid shall either give, sell or *truck* any commoditie whatsoever without licence from their Masters, during the time of their service under pain of Fine , or corporal punishment at the discretion of the Court as the offence shall deserve .

2 And that all workmen shall work the whole day allowing convenient time for food and rest .

3 It is also ordered that when any servants shall run from their masters , or any other Inhabitants shall privily goe away with suspicion of ill intentions , it shall be lawfull for the next Magistrate , or the Constable and two of the chief Inhabitants where no Magistrate is to presse men and boats or pinnaces at the publick charge to pursue such persons by Sea or Land and bring them back by force of Arms .

4 It is also ordered by the Authoritie aforesaid , that the Free-men of everie town may from time to time as occasion shall require agree amongst themselves about the prizes, and rates of all workmens labours and servants wages . And everie person inhabiting in any town , whether workman, labourer or servant shall be bound to the same rates which the said Freemen, or the greater part shall binde themselves unto : and whosoever shall exceed those rates so agreed shall be punished by the discretion of the Court of that Shire , according to the qualitie and measure of the offence . And if any town shall have cause of complaint against the Freemen of any other town for allowing greater rates, or wages then themselves , the Quarter Court of that Shire shall from time to time set order therin .

5 And for servants and workmens wages , it is ordered, that they may be paid in corn , to be valued by two indifferent Freemen, chosen the one by the Master, the other by the servant or workman , who also are to have respect to the value of the work or service , and if they cannot agree then a third man shall be chosen by the next Magistrate , or if no Magistrate be in the town then by the next Constable , unles the parties agree the price themselves . Provided if any servant or workman agree for any
particular

particular payment, then to be payd *in specie*, or consideration for default therin. And for all other payments in corn, if the parties cannot agree they shall choof two indifferent men, and if they cannot agree then a third as before.

6 It is ordered, and by this Court declared, that if any servant shall flee from the tyrannie and crueltie of his, or her Master to the houfe of any Freeman of the fame town, they shall be there protected and fufteined till due order be taken for their releif. Provided due notice therof be speedily given to their Master from whom they fled, and to the next Magistrate or Conftable where the partie fo fled is harboured.

7 Also that no servant shall be put off for above a year to any other, neither in the life time of their Master, nor after their death by their Executors or Administrators, unles it be by consent of Authorite affembled in fome Court, or two Affiftants: otherwise all, and everie such Affignment to be void in Law.

8 And that if any man fmite out the eye, or tooth of his man-fervant, or maid-fervant; or otherwife maim, or much disfigure them (unles it be by meer cafualtie) he shall let them goe free from his fervice, and shall allow fuch farther recompence as the Court shall adjudge him.

9 And all servants that have ferved diligently and faithfully to the benefit of their Masters feven years shall not be fent away emptie: and if any have been unfaithfull, negligent, or unprofitable in their fervice, notwithstanding the good ufage of their Masters, they shall not be difmiffed till they have made fatisfaction according to the judgement of Authoritie. [1630 1633 1635 1636 1641] *See Oppreffion*

## *Militarie Affairs.*

FORASMUCH as the wife, and well mannaging the Militia of this Commonwealth is a matter of great concernment, therefore that it may be carried an end with the utmoft fafety and certaintie for the beft benefit of the Countrie, it is ordered by this Court and Authoritie therof;

That henceforth there shall be one Sergeant Major of everie Regiment chosen by the trained foldiers of everie Town in each Shire, not only Freemen, but all others that have taken, and shall take the Oath of fidelitie (except unfetled perfons) who upon *Warrant* from the General Court, or Sergeant Major General shall meet together in their feveral Towns from time to time, and give in their Votes for fuch a man, or men as they shall judge fit for the Office of Sergeant Major of that Regiment, and where no Magiftrate is in the Town, or neer hand to give Oath to fuch foldiers as defire to take the fame before the Election, power is heerby given to the Captain, or in defect therof to the next cheif Officer of the Company in all Towns to adminifter the faid Oath of fidelitie; who shall certifie the next Court of that County the names of all foldiers fo fworn to be recorded there: which Votes of the whole Company shall be fealed up, and delivered to one, or both the Deputies of the faid Town, or any other Freeman that the Town shall appoint to carie them to the Shire town of each County at fuch time as the *Warrant* shall direct, and there before one or two of the neereft Magiftrates to open the *Proxies* with the faid Deputies or Freemen. And he that shall have the greater number of Votes, being a Freeman, shall be prefented by one of the faid Magiftrates of each Shire unto the Sergeant Major General within one week after the Election, who shall enftall, confirm and eftablish each Sergeant Major in his place for one year, who shall alfo retein their place and power, till a new Election be made by the General Court, or otherwife according to this Order. And to avoid the vacancy of a place fo neceffarie for time to come, it is ordered, that if any such Officer leave their places, or be removed out of them the Sergeant Major General for the time being shall within one month at the fartheft after fuch a change fend forth his *Warrants* to each town in the fame Shire to make choif of one or more for Majors according to the form afore-mentioned.

2 And it is farther ordered, that everie Sergeant Major not only hath libertie, but also

F 2

also is heerby injoyned once everie year at leaſt, and oftener upon any needfull occaſion, or command from the Major General to draw forth his Regiment into one convenient place, and there to put everie Captain and Officer of their Companyes in their
places, and to inſtruct them in their duties according to the rules of militarie Diſciplin,
and to exerciſe his Regiment, whether it ſhall conſiſt of Horſe, Pikes or Musketiers
according to his beſt skill and abilities as if he were to lead them forth againſt an enemie. And farther, that everie Sergeant Major not only hath power, but is injoyned
by the Court twice everie year to ſend forth his *Warrants* or *Summons* to require the
chief Officers of each Company in his Regiment to meet at ſuch time and place as he
ſhall appoint, and there, with them to confer, and give in command ſuch Orders as
ſhall by them be judged meet for the better ordering and ſetling their particular Companyes in militarie Exerciſes: and that theſe Officers of particular Companyes ſhall
bring with them a note from the *Rolls* of their ſeverall Clerks of the names of ſuch in
their ſeveral Companyes as remain delinquents, and have not given ſatisfaction to the
Captain, or cheif Officers of their Companyes for all defects either in their arms, amunition, appearances, watches, offences, or the like. And that the Sergeant Major
with the conſent of thoſe Officers, then met together, ſhall impoſe ſuch Fines or Penalties according to Law upon delinqents as ſhall be judged equal, and ſhall give order to
the Clerks of the ſeverall Bands to take *diſtreſſe* for the ſame, within one month after
ſuch order, if before, they give not ſatisfaction.

3 *And becauſe we obſerve and underſtand many defects to be in making appearances, in Arms unfit for ſervice and otherwiſe, we order that it ſhall be inſerted into
the Oath of everie Clerk of the Band as followeth,*

First, that upon everie training day twice, once in the forenoon, as alſo in
the after-noon at ſuch time as the Captain, or cheif Officer that is then in the field ſhall
appoint to call, or cauſe to be called over the Liſt of the names of all the ſoldiers; and
that he ſhall give his attendance in the field all the day (except he have ſpecial leave
from his Captain, or chief Officer) for the taking notice of any defect by the abſence
of ſoldiers, and other offences that doe often fall out in the time of Exerciſe, as well
as in the calling over of the *Rolls*.

Secondly, that twice everie year, at leaſt, he ſhall view all the Arms and Amunition of the Band to ſee if they be all according to Law: to which end, by direction
of the Captain, or chief Officer of the Band he ſhall give notice to the ſoldiers that
upon ſuch a training day appointed, they be required to bring (in the fore-noon) all their
Arms and Amunition into the field that is required by Law; where they ſhall be approved or diſ-allowed by the judgements of the ſaid chief Officers then in the field.
Alſo, the Clerk ſhall ſee that everie *Musketier* have one pound of powder, twenty
*bullets* and two fathom of *match*, with *Musket, Sword, Bandeliers* and *Reſt*, upon the
penalty of ten ſhillings for everie defect. And to levie five ſhillings forfeit upon all
ſoldiers that ſhall be abſent from training, or defective in watching and warding, except they be diſcharged, or their Fine mittigated in any the particulars afore-mentioned,
by the chief Officers of the Company. And that the Clerk as often as he ſhall ſee
occaſion is injoyned to uſe all diligence to view everie ones Arms, whether they be com-
pleatly furniſhed with all Arms and Amunition that the Law requireth.

Thirdly, he ſhall ſee that all Inhabitants, as well Sea-men as others have Arms
in their houſes fit for ſervice, with *Powder, Bullets, Match* and other amunition as
other ſoldiers: and that Fiſhermen, Ship-carpenters and all others, not exempted by
Law (except *Deacons*, who heerby are freed from watching and warding) ſhall watch
or provide a ſufficient Watch-man in their room, and to train twice a year according
to the Order.

Fourthly, that the militarie Officers of each Company ſhall appoint what arms
everie ſoldier ſhall ſerve with, ſo that there be two thirds *Muskets*, and thoſe which
ſerve with *Pikes* to have their *Corſlets* and *Head-pieces*.

Fiftly, that the Clerk ſhall within one week after everie training day truly
present

---

**Everie Regi-
ment to train
once a year at
com: of the
Major Gener:**

**The chief
Officers of
everie Regim:
to meet twice
a year by war:
from § Major
for what ends**

**puniſh delin-
quents.**

**Clerk of Band,
his duty.**

**milit: Officers
appoint what
Arms.**

present a List of the names of all that are delinquents, and of the defects of the Band to the Captain, or chief Officer of the Company, that he may have them all in a readines to carrie with him when the Major of the Regiment shall appoint his meeting, which have not before given satisfaction at home, according to Law. And the Order that gives power to Magistrates to releas upon non-appearance is heerby repealed.

Sixtly, that the Clerk (without all partialitie) shall demand, and receive all **Fines**, which if any shall refuse to pay, then he shall make *distresse* upon the goods of all such persons as first by the chief Officer of their own Company at home, or by the Major and chief Officers met together *(as before mentioned)* shall be judged delinquents. And that the Clerk with the advise of the chief Officers of their own company shall speedily lay out all Fines received either in *Ensigne*, *Drum*, *Halberds*, candle, or wood for their Court of Guard, or to provide *Powder* or *Arms* for the poorer sort, or otherwise for the use of the Company. Provided, that no Clerk of the Band shall stand charged with the execution of any former Order by vertue of his said Office, other then such as are committed to his care and charge by this present Order.

Lastly, if any Clerk of a Band, chosen, shall refuse either to accept the place, or to take his Oath, he shall pay to the use of the Company fourty shillings, and the Company shall choos another, and all that refuse the said Place, or Oath as before shall pay fourty shillings a peece till one doth accept the Place. And he that doth hold the Place shall have a fourth part of the Fines for his labour.

**4** *For the militarie Watch in all Towns it is ordered;*

First, that the Watch shall be set and have their charge by the direction of the chief militarie Officers of that place, half an hour after sun-setting.

Secondly, that the Watch being set [which shall stand double, a *Pike* and a *Musket* together] shall examin all persons that they shall meet withall within the compasse of their Watch or Round: and all such as they suspect they shall carry to the Court of Guard there to be kept untill the morning, and before they be dismissed they shall carrie them to their chief Officers to be examined and proceeded with according to Law.

Thirdly, if the Centinel, or Watch shall meet with such persons as shall prove too strong for them, or by their carriage shall give just cause of suspicion, or will not submit to their command, or if they shall either draw upon them, or offer any such affronts, in words or actions as shall put them in fear or hazzard of their lives, they shall charge their *Pike* and discharge their *Musket* upon them, and return with speed to their Court of Guard and raise an Alarm. Provided alwayes that in times of peace when the Council of war, or the chief Officers of any Company shall not apprehend danger by the neernes of an enemie, it shall not be in the libertie of any Centinel to hazzard the killing of any person, or persons, except in his own necessarie defence, but if the cause require it he shall raise an Alarm, or retire to the Court of Guard.

**5** *For the well ordering of the militarie Companies and affairs throughout this Jurisdiction it is ordered by this Court and Authoritie therof;*

That the militarie Officers of each Company upon three or four dayes warning or more, in any publick Meeting, or otherwise in their own Town shall from time to time appoint the dayes for training their Companies; so as there be eight dayes appointed for the same everie year, and none of them to be in the fift or sixth months.

*Also, it is ordered, for ease of all soldiers when, and where the Regiments are exercised,* That so many dayes as they shall necessarily expend by the injunction of the Sergeant Major, both in marching to and from exercise at General trainings, shall be deducted out of their eight dayes annual trainings.

And that all Magistrats, Deputies, and Officers of court, Elders and Deacons, the President, Fellows, Students and Officers of *Harvard-Colledge*, and all professed School-masters, allowed by any two Magistrates, the Treasurer, Auditor general and Surveyor General of the Arms, Publick Notaries, Physitians and Chirurgions,

F 3                                                                            allowed

allowed by two Magiftrates, Mafters of fhipps and other veffels above twenty tunnes, Millers and conftant Heards-men, and fuch other as by any Court fhall be difcharged, either for bodily infirmity, or other reafonable caufe fhall be exempt from ordinary trainings, and from watchings and wardings but not their fons or fervants, fave one fervant of everie Magiftrate and Teaching Elder allowed exemption : and all fuch as keep families at remote Farms fhall not be compellable to fend their fervants to watch and ward in Towns. And the fons, and houfhold fervants of the Major General for the time being fhall be exercifed by his own order, and not otherwife compellable to attend the ordinary trainings. But all perfons whatfoever exempted as aforefaid, except Magiftrates and Teaching Elders fhall be provided of Arms and Amunition, as other men are.

6 Alfo that everie foldier Lifted in any trayned Band, having taken the Oath of fidelitie, and everie Freeman (though not fo lifted) fhall have his Vote in nomination of militarie Officers of that Company, or Town whereof he is, provided they be Freemen. And everie Captain, Lievtenant and Enfigne fo nominated fhall be prefented to the next County Court to be allowed.

7 And if any perfon who is by Law to provide Arms or Amunition cannot purchafe them by fuch means as he hath, he fhall bring to the Clerk fo much corn, or other merchantable goods as by apprizement of the faid Clerk and two others of the Company (wherof one to be chofen by the partie) fhall be adjudged of greater value, by a fift part then fuch Arms or Amunition is of, he fhall be excufed of the penaltie for want of Arms (but not for want of appearance) untill he be provided. And the Clerk fhall indeavour to furnifh him fo foon as may be by fale of fuch goods fo depofited, rendring the partie the overplus. But if any perfon fhall not be able to provide himfelfe Arms or Amunition through meer povertie, if he be fingle, he fhall be put to fervice by fome Magiftrate, & the Conftable fhall provide him Arms and Amunition, and fhall appoint him when, and with whom to earn it out.

8 Alfo, that no *Musket* fhall be allowed for fervice under baftard musket bore, and not under three foot nine inches in length, nor any piece above four foot three inches long. And everie fuch foldier fhall be furnifhed with a priming wyer, Worm, Scourer and Mould, fitted to the bore of his *Musket* : and everie foldier with a Snap-fack.

9 It is alfo ordered by the Authoritie aforefaid; that upon any militarie expedition upon occafion of an enemie all Smiths and other needfull Workmen fhall attend the repairing of Arms, and other neceffaries : for which they fhall not refufe fuch pay as the Countrie affords upon pain of five pounds for everie fuch neglect. And for fuch neglect at any other time more then ten dayes, to forfeit for everie fuch offence ten fhillings.

10 Alfo, power is given to the Surveyor general to fell any of the common Arms, when he feeth occafion.

11 And everie Town which fhall have any arms or amunition belonging to the common Store of the Town fhall provide a meet place to keep the fame in; and fhall fafely preferve the fame upon pain of ten fhillings for everie weeks default therin.

12 Alfo, the militarie Officers of everie Company in fuch places and at fuch times as they fhall apprehend danger from an enemie, fhall have power to order the foldiers of their Companies what arms to bring to the Meeting-houfes, at the times of the publick Affemblies : and to take order for the fecuring the arms and amunition at remote Farms. Alfo, in everie Company fome under Officer fhall be appointed by the cheif Commander to exercife fuch children as by their Parents and Mafters allowance fhall refort to the Traynings.

13 It is alfo ordered, that in the times of danger the watches & wards fhal be fet by the militarie Officers in fuch places as they fhall judge moft convenient, and if any man fhall fhoot off a gun after fuch watch is fet (except in cafe of Alarm) he fhall forfeit to the Treafurie fourty fhillings. *See Watches.*

14 And

---

**Marginal notes:**

Any Court may difcharge upon caufe

whofe fons & fervants fhal be exempted.

Major Ge.

perfons exempt that have Arms except.

who have vote in election of mil: Officers to be allowed by the next Cou: court

where Arms cañot be had

want of ability to bring Arms

affize of muskets & their furniture

Snap-fack.

Smiths &c: at ted repair for country pay &c: Penalty five pounds. Pen: ten fhil:

Suveyor Ge: may fell coun try Arms Town Arms fafely kept pen: 10 fs. the week.

Bring arms to Meet: houfes

Secur: Arms at Farms Exercifing youth &c:

mili: watches in time of danger. Shooting in night Penalty 40 fs.

14 And for an Alarm, either the diſtinct diſcharge of three *Muskets* or the continued beat of the *Drum*, or the fyring of a *Beacon*, or diſcharge of a Piece of *Ordinance* and two *Muskets* after it, or any of theſe in the night; or the ſending of a meſſenger on purpoſe to give notice of an enemie at hand ſhall be accounted a general Alarm, which everie trayned Soldier is to take immediately, on pain of five pounds. And beſides the ſaid general Alarm there ſhall be a ſpecial Alarm for the Town *viz:* one *Musket* diſcharged, which the Centinell ſhall anſwer by going to all the houſes in his quarters and crying arm, arm. And if the danger appear the chief Officers may either ſtrengthen their quarters, or give a general Alarm; and they ſhal ſet their Centinels or Courts of guard where they ſhall judge moſt convenient: and upon certain intelligence of an enemie at one Town, the Commanders of the three next Towns ſhall repair thither with a ſufficient company according to the intelligence given them of the enemies ſtrength.

15 Also any three chief Officers of each company ſhall heerby have power to puniſh ſuch Soldiers as ſhall commit any diſorder, or contempt upon any day, or time of militarie exerciſe, or upon any Watch or Ward by *Stocks, Bilb023* or any other uſuall military puniſhment, or by Fine, not exceeding twenty ſhillings, or may commit ſuch offender to the Conſtable to be carried before ſome Magiſtrate, who may binde him over to the next Court of that Shire if the cauſe ſo require, or comit him to priſon.

16 It is heerby declared, that it belongeth to the place of the Governour for the time being to be General of all the militarie Forces. But when occaſion of ſervice ſhal be againſt an enemie, the General Court or ſtanding Council may appoint ſome other to that Office untill the Forces rayſed ſhall be disbanded.

17 Laſtly, every Town ſhall provide a ſufficient Watch-houſe before the laſt of the fifth month next upon pain of five pounds. [1645 1647] *See Council.*

### Mills, Millers.

IT is ordered by this Court and Authoritie therof, that no Miller ſhall take above the ſixteenth part of the corn he grindes. And that everie Miller ſhall have allwayes ready in his mill, weights and skoals provided at his own charges, to weigh corn to and from mill, if men deſire it. [1635 1638]

### Monopolies.

IT is ordered, decreed and by this Court declared; that there ſhall be no *Monopolies* graunted or allowed amongſt us, but of ſuch new inventions that are profitable for the Countrie, and that for a ſhort time. [1641]

### Oaths, Subſcription

IT is ordered and decreed, and by this Court declared; that no man ſhall be urged to take any oath, or ſubſcribe any Articles, Covenants, or remonſtrance of publick and civil nature but ſuch as the General Court hath conſidered, allowed and required. And that no oath of Magiſtrate, Counceller or any other Officer ſhall binde him any farther, or longer then he is reſident, or reputed an Inhabitant of this Juriſdictiõ [1641]

### Oppreſſion

FOR avoyding ſuch miſcheifs as may follow by ſuch ill diſpoſed perſons as may take libertie to oppreſſe and wrong their neighbours, by taking exceſſive wages for work, or unreaſonable prizes for ſuch neceſſarie merchandizes or other commodities as ſhall paſſe from man to man, it is ordered, That if any man ſhall offend in any of the ſaid caſes he ſhall be puniſhed by Fine, or Impriſonment according to the qualitie of the offence, as the Court to which he is preſented upon lawfull tryall & conviction ſhall adjudge. [1635]

### Payments.

IT is ordered by the Authoritie of this Court, that all payments of Debt, Legacyes and Fines ſhall be ſatisfied in kinde according to covenant or ingagement, or in default therof in corn, cattle, fiſh or other comodities at ſuch rates as this Court ſhall appoint from time to time, or by apprizement of indifferent men to be appointed by the Officer one, and either partie one. Provided that in all and everie the caſes aforeſaid

aforesaid all just damages shall be satisfied together with the debt, or other payment to the partie for not paying in kinde according to the bargain. [1640]

### Pipe-staves.

WHERAS *information hath come to this Court from divers forrein parts of the insufficiencie of our Pipe-staves in regard especially of worm holes, wherby the commoditie is like to be prohibited in those parts, to the great damage of the Countrie; it is therfore ordered and enacted by the Authoritie of this Court,*

That the Select-men of *Boston* and *Charlstown* and of all other towns in this Jurisdiction where Pipe-staves use to be shipped; shall forthwith, and so from time to time as need shall require nominate two men of each town, skilfull in that commoditie, and such as can attend that service to be Viewers of Pipe-staves; who so chosen, shall by the Constable be convented before some Magistrate, to be sworn diligently and faithfully to view and search all such Pipe-staves as are to be transported to any parts of *Spain*, *Portugal*, or within either of their Dominions, or elsewhere to be used for making of tight cask, who shall cast bye all such as they shall judge not merchantable both in respect of worm-holes and due assize *viz.* that are not in length four foot & half, in breadth three inches and half without sap, in thicknes three quarters of an inch, & not more or lesse then an eight part of an inch then three quarters thick: well, and even hewed and sufficient for that use. And they or some one of them shall at all times upon request give attendance; & they shall enter in a book the number of all such merchantable Pipe-staves as they shall approve, and for whom.

And if any man shall put aboard any Ship, or other vessel any Pipe-staves other then shall be so searched and approved, to the end to be transported to any part of *Spain* or *Portugal*, except they should be shipped for dry cask, he shall forfeit the same whole parcell or the value therof; and the said Viewers shall be allowed two shillings for everie thousand of Pipe-staves which they shall so search, as well the refuse as the merchantable, to be paid by him that sets them a work.

And if any Master or other Officer of any Ship, or other vessel shall receive into such Ship or vessel any parcel of Pipe-staves to be transported into any of the said Dominions which shall not be searched, and allowed as merchantable, and so certified by a note under the hand of one of the said Viewers such Master shall forfeit for everie thousand of Pipe-staves so unduly received five pounds; except he can procure one of the said Viewers to come aboard and search such staves as they shall be delivered into the Ship.

Provided, cask staves or other red oak staves may be transported into those parts, which may be of good use for drye cask. And that there be the like Officers chosen for *Salem* and *Pescataway*, where staves may be shipped away as well as from *Boston* [1646]

### Poor.

IT is ordered by this Court and Authoritie therof; that any Shire Court, or any two Magistrates out of Court shall have power to determin all differences about lawfull setling, and providing for poor persons: and shall have power to dispose of all unsetled persons into such towns as they shall judge to be most fit for the maintainance, and imployment of such persons and families, for the ease of the Countrie. [1639]

### Pound, Pound breach.

FOR prevention, and due recompence of damages in corn fields, and other inclosures, done by swine and cattle, it is ordered by this Court and Authoritie therof;

That there shall be one sufficient Pound, or more made and maintained in everie Town and Village within this jurisdiction, for the impounding of all such swine and cattle as shall be found in any corn field or other inclosure. And who so impounds any swine or cattle shall give present notice to the Owner, if he be known, otherwise they shal be cryed at the two next Lectures or Markets, and if swine or cattle escape out of pound the owners, if known, shal pay all damages according to law. [1645 1647]

2 *Wheras*

**[marginal notes:]**

Searchers of Pipe-staves

sworn.

Assize of Pipe-staves

attend, Register.

Owners shipping ûlawfull Pipestaves. Due cask Forfeit. Searchers allowance.

Master, shipping ûlawfull Pipe-staves

Forfeit,

Dry cask.

To be setled where, & by whom.

2 *Wheras imp*[ounding] *ounding of cattle in case of trespasse hath been alwayes found both needfull and profitable, and* [al] *l all breaches about the same very offensive and injurious, it is therfore ordered by this Cour*[t] *t and Authoritie therof;*

That if any perso[n] n shall resist, or rescue any cattle going to the *Pound*, or shall by any way or means co[n]vey them out of *pound* or other custodie of the Law, whereby the partie wronged may [l]ose his damages, and the Law be deluded, that in case of meer *rescues* the partie so offen[d]ing shall forfeit to the Treasurie fourty shillings. And in case of pound breach five [p]ounds, and shall also pay all damages to the partie wronged, and if in the *rescues* any bodily harm be done to the person of any man or other, they may have remedie against the *Rescuers*; and if either be done by any not of abilitie to answer the Forfeiture and damages aforesaid, they shall be openly whipped, by *Warrant* from any Magistrate before whom the offender is convicted, in the Town or Plantation where the offence was committed, not exceeding twenty stripes for the meer *rescues* or pound breach. And for all damages to the partie they shall satisfie by service as in case of theft. And if it appear there were any procurement of the Owner of the cattle therunto, and that they were *Abbettors* therin, they shall also pay Forfeiture and damages as if themselves had done it. [1647]

Rescues simpl
Fine.
Pound breach. Fine. Rescues with Battery.
Whipped. one Magistr:
damage satisfied by serv:

*Powder.*

IT is ordered by this Court and the Authoritie therof, that whosoever shall transport any *Gun-powder* out of this Jurisdiction without licence first obtained from some two of the Magistrates, shall forfeit for everie such offence all such *powder* as shall be transporting or transported, or the value therof. And that there may be noe defect for want of an Officer to take care therabouts, this Court, the Court of Assistants, or any Shire Court shall appoynt meet persons from time to time in all needfull places, who have heerby power graunted them, to search all persons and vessels that are, or any way shall be suspicious to them to be breakers of the Court Order in this respect, and what they finde in any vessel, or hands without order, as aforesaid, to keep the one half to their own use, in recompence of their pains and vigilancy, the other half forthwith to deliver to the Treasurer. [1645] *See Indians.*

Searchers for powder.
Forfeit divided,

*Prescriptions.*

IT is ordered, decreed, and by this Court declared; that no *Custom* or *Prescription* shall ever prevail amongst us in any moral case [our meaning is] to maintein any thing that can be proved to be morally sinfull by the Word of God. [1641]

Not for evil.

*Prisoners, Prisons.*

IT is ordered by Authoritie of this Court; that such malefactors as are committed to any common *Prison* shall be conveyed thither at their own charge, if they be able, otherwise at the charge of the Country. [1646] *See Marshal.*

Their charges.

*Profane swearing.*

IT is ordered, and by this Court decreed, that if any person within this Jurisdiction shall *swear* rashly and vainly either by the holy Name of God, or any other oath, he shall forfeit to the common Treasurie for everie such severall offence ten shillings. And it shall be in the power of any Magistrate by *Warrant* to the Constable to call such person before him, and upon sufficient proof to passe sentence, and levie the said penaltie according to the usuall order of Justice. And if such person be not able, or shall utterly refuse to pay the aforesaid Fine, he shal be committed to the *Stocks* there to continue, not exceeding three hours, and not lesse then one hour. [1646]

Fine, 10 s.
Stocks.

*Protestation contra Remonstrance.*

IT is ordered, decreed, and by this Court declared; that it is, and shall be the libertie of any member, or members of any Court, Council or civil Assemblie in cases of making or executing any Order or Law that properly concerneth Religion, or any cause Capital, or Wars, or subscription to any publick Articles, or Remonstrance in case they cannot in judgement and conscience consent to that way the major Vote or Suffrage goes, to make their *contra-Remonstrance* or *Protestation* in speech or writing, and upon their request, to have their dissent recorded in the *Rolls* of that Court, so it be done

Freedom of dissent.

done christianly and respectively, for the manner, and the dissent only be entred without the reasons therof for avoyding tediousnes. [1641]

## Punishment

IT is ordered, decreed, and by this Court declared; that no man shall be twice sentenced by civil Justice for one and the same Crime, Offence or Trespasse. And for bodily punishments, wee allow amongst us none that are in-humane, barbarous or cruel. [1641] *See Appearance, Torture.*

*Once for one offence. None inhumane.*

## Rates, Fines.

WHERAS much wrong hath been done to the Countrie by the negligence of Constables in not gathering such Levies as they have received Warrants from the Treasurer, during their Office, it is therefore ordered;

That if any Constable shall not have gathered the Levies committed to his charge by the Treasurer then being, during the time of his Office, that he shall notwithstanding the expiration of his Office have power to levie by distresse all such Rates and Levies. And if he bring them not in to the old Treasurer according to his Warrants, the Treasurer shall distrein such Constables goods for the same. And if the Treasurer shall not so distrein the Constable, he shall be answerable to the Countrie for the same. And if the Constable be not able to make payment, it shall be lawfull for the Treasurer, old or new, respectively to distrein any man, or men of that Town where the Constables are unable for all arrerages of Levies. And that man, or men upon petition to the General Court shall have order to collect the same again equally of the Town, with his just damages for the same. [1640] *See Charges publ: Constable, Ecclesiasticall: Fines.*

*The Const: levie Rates after his Offi: is expired. If defective ý Treasurer distr: Const: goods else himself payeth Town pays for Const: remedy where one suffers for ý town*

## Records.

WHERAS Records of the evidence and reasons wherupon the Verdict and Judgement in cases doth passe, being duly entred, and kept would be of good use (for president to posteritie, and to such as shall have just cause to have their causes reviewed), it is therfore ordered by this Court and the Authoritie therof,

That henceforth everie Judgement given in any Court, with all the substantial reasons shall be recorded in a book, to be kept to posteritie. And that in all Towns within this Jurisdiction where there is no Magistrate, the three men appointed, and sworn to end small causes not exceeding fourty shillings value shall from time to time keep a true Record of all such Causes as shall come before them to be determined. And that everie Plaintiffe shall pay one shilling six pence for everie Cause so tryed, toward the charge therof. And that the times of their meetings be published, that all may take notice therof that are concerned therin. And also that in all Towns where a Magistrate shall end such small Causes, he shall keep the like Record, and take the like Fee of one shilling sixpence.

*presidents for posteritie*

*Tryalls by three men their records.*

*& Fees.*

2 Also, it is ordered by the Authoritie aforesaid that where parties dwell in severall Towns it shall be in the libertie of the Plaintiffe in which Town to trie his Action.

*One Magistr: to record*

*small causes tryable where*

3 Also, that heerafter the Clerk of the Writs in severall Towns shall record all Births and Deaths of persons in their Towns; and that for everie Birth and Death they so record they are allowed the sum of three pence: who shall yearly deliver in to the Recorder of the Court belonging to the Jurisdiction where they live a true Transcript therof, together with so many pence as there are Births and Deaths to be recorded, under the penaltie of fourty shillings for everie such neglect.

*Town records, kept by Clerk of writs his Fee. Transcript recorded in Cou: Courts*

4 And it is ordered by the Authoritie aforesaid that all Parents, Masters of servants, Executors and Administrators respectively shall bring in, to the Clerks of the Writs in their severall Towns the names of such persons belonging to them, or any of them, as shall either be born, or dye. And also, that everie new married man shall likewise bring in a Certificat of his marriage under the hand of the Magistrate which married him to the said Clerk of the Writs, who shall under the penaltie of twenty shillings deliver as aforesaid unto the Recorder a Certificat under his hand, with a penie a name, as well for the recording of marriages as the rest. And for each neglect the person to whom

*Births, deaths marriages certified.*

whom it doth belong shall forfeit as followeth *viz:* if any person shall neglect to bring in a *note* or *Certificat* as aforesaid, together with three pence a name to the said *Clerk* of the *Writs* to be recorded more then one month after such Birth, Death, or Marriage he shall then pay six pence to the said *Clerk* : if he neglect two months twelve pence, if three months five shillings. All which forfeits shall be returned into the Treasury. Also, the Grand-Jurors may present all neglects of this Order.

5 It is ordered, decreed, and by this Court declared; that everie man shall have libertie to record in the publick *Rolls* of any Court, any testimonie given upon oath in the same Court, or before two Assistants; or any *Deed* or *Evidence* legally confirmed, there to remain *in perpetuam rei memoriam*. And that everie Inhabitant of the Countrie shal have free libertie to search and view any *Rolls, Records* or *registers* of any Court or Office except of the Council. And to have a *Transcript* or *exemplification* therof written, examined and signed by the hand of the Officer of the Office, paying the appointed Fees therefore. Also, everie Action between partie and partie and proceedings against delinquents in *criminal* Causes shall be briefly and distinctly entred in the *rolls* of everie Court by the *Recorder* therof, that such Actions be not afterwards brought again to the vexation of any man. [1639 1642 1643 1644 1647] *See Conveyances fraudulent.*

## Replevin

IT is ordered, decreed and by this Court declared; that everie man shall have libertie to *replevie* his cattle or goods impounded, distreined, seized or extended, unles it be upon Execution after judgement, and in payment of Fines. Provided he puts in good securitie to prosecute the *Replevin*, and to satisfie such demand as his Adversarie shall recover against him in Law. [1641] *See Clerk of Writs, Presidents.*

## Schools.

IT being one chief project of that old deluder, *Satan*, to keep men from the knowledge of the Scriptures, *as in former times keeping them in an unknown tongue*, so in these later times by perswading from the use of Tongues, that so at least the true sense and meaning of the Originall might be clowded with false glosses of Saint-seeming-deceivers; and that Learning may not be buried in the graves of our fore-fathers in Church and Commonwealth, the Lord assisting our indeavours: it is therfore ordered by this Court and Authoritie therof;

That everie Township in this Jurisdiction, after the Lord hath increased them to the number of fifty Housholders shall then forthwith appoint one within their Town to teach all such children as shall resort to him to write and read, whose wages shall be paid either by the Parents or Masters of such children, or by the Inhabitants in general by way of supply, as the major part of those that order the *prudentials* of the Town shall appoint. Provided that those which send their children be not oppressed by paying much more then they can have them taught for in other Towns.

2 And it is farther ordered, that where any Town shall increase to the number of one hundred Families or Housholders they shal set upon a Grammar-School, the Masters therof being able to instruct youth so far as they may be fitted for the Universitie. And if any Town neglect the performance heerof above one year then everie such town shall pay five pounds *per annum* to the next such School, till they shall perform this Order. [1647]

## Secresie.

IT is ordered, decreed, and by this Court declared; that no Magistrate, Juror, Officer or other man shall be bound to inform, present or reveal any private crime or offence wherin there is no perill or danger to this Colonie, or any member therof, when any necessarie tye of conscience, grounded on the word of God bindes him to secresie; unles it be in case of testimonie lawfully required. [1641] *See Oath Grand-Jurie.*

## Secretarie.

TO the end that all *Acts* of the General Court may be amply, distinctly and more exactly drawn up, ingrossed and recorded, and the busines of all perticular Courts may also be more duly entred, and severally recorded for publick good, it is ordered by this Court and the Authoritie therof;

That henceforth there shall be one able, judicious man chosen at the Court of Election *annually* (as other general Officers are chosen) for *Secretarie* of the General Court. And that all other Courts shal choof their own Officers frō time to time. [1647]

### Ships, Ship-masters.

WHERAS *now the Countrie is in hand with the building of Ships, which is a busines of great importance for the Common good, and therfore sutable care is to be taken that it be well performed according to the commendable course of England and other places, it is therefore ordered by this Court and the Authoritie therof;*

That when any Ship is to be built within this Jurisdiction, or any vessell above thirty tuns, the Owner, or builder in his absence shall before they begin to plank, repair to the Governour or Deputie-Governour, or any two Magistrates upon the penaltie of ten pounds, who shall appoint some able man to survey the work and workmen from

time to time as is usual in England. And the same so appointed shall have such libertie and power as belongs to his office. And if any Ship-carpenter shall not upon his advice reform and amend any thing which he shall finde to be amisse, then upon complaint to the Governour or Deputie Governour or any other two Magistrates, they shall appoint two of the most sufficient Ship-carpenters of this Jurisdiction, and shall autho-

rize them from time to time as need shall require to take view of everie such ship, and all works thereto belonging, and to see that it be performed and caried on according to the rules of their Art. And for this end an oath shall be administred to them to

be faithfull and indifferent between the Owner and the Workmen; and their charges shall be born by such as shall be found in default. And those Viewers shall have power to cause any bad timbers, or other insufficient work or materials to be taken out, and amended at the charge of them through whose default it grows. [1641 1647]

2 It is ordered by the Authoritie of this Court, that all ships which come for trading

only, from other parts, shall have free accesse into our Harbours, and quiet riding there, and free libertie to depart without any molestation by us: they paying all such duties, and charges required by law in the Countrie, as others doe. [1645]

### Straies.

IT is ordered by this Court and the Authoritie therof; that whosoever shall take up any straie beast, or finde any goods lost wherof the owner is not known, he shall give notice therof to the Constable of the same Town within six dayes, who shall enter the same in a book and take order that it be cryed at their next Lecture day, or general Town-meeting upon three severall dayes. And if it be above twenty shillings value, at the next Market or two next towns publick meetings, where no Market is within ten miles, upon pain that the partie so finding, and the said Constable having such notice and failing to do as is heer appointed, to forfeit either of them for such default one third part of the value of such straie, or lost goods.

And if the finder shall not give notice as aforesaid within one month, or if he keep it more then three months, and shall not apprize it by indifferent men, and also record it with the *Recorder* of the County Court where it is found, he shall then forfeit

the full value therof. And if the Owner appears within one year after such publication he shall have restitution of the same, or the value therof paying all necessarie charg-

es, and to the Constable for his care and paines as one of the next Magistrates or the deputed three men of the Town shall adjudge. And if no Owner appear within the time prefixed the said *Stray* or lost goods shall be to the use of the finder, paying to the Constable ten shillings, or the fifth part of the value of such *Straie* or goods lost, at the finders choice.

Provided that everie such finder shall put, and keep from time to time a With or Wreath about the neck of all such stray beast within one month after such finding, upon penaltie of losing all his charges that shall arise about it afterwards. Provided also, that

that if any Owner or other fhall take off fuch With or Wreath, or take away fuch beaft before he have difcharged according to this Order, he fhall forfeit the full value of the thing apprized as aforefaid, to the ufe of the finder, as is before expreffed. [1647]

### Strangers.

IT is ordered by this Court and the Authoritie therof; that no Town or perfon fhal receive any ftranger reforting hither with intent to refide in this Jurifdiction, nor fhall allow any Lot or Habitation to any, or entertain any fuch above three weeks, except fuch perfon fhall have allowance under the hand of fome one Magiftrate, upon pain of everie Town that fhall give, or fell any Lot or Habitation to any not fo licenced fuch Fine to the Countrie as that County Court fhall impofe, not exceeding fifty pounds, nor leffe then ten pounds. And of everie perfon receiving any fuch for longer time then is heer expreffed or allowed, in fome fpecial cafes as before, or in cafe of entertainment of friends reforting from other parts of this Country in amitie with us, fhall forfeit as aforefaid, not exceeding twenty pounds, nor leffe then four pounds: and for everie month after fo offending, fhal forfeit as aforefaid not exceeding ten pounds, nor leffe then fourty fhillings. Alfo, that all Conftables fhall inform the Courts of new commers which they know to be admitted without licence, from time to time. [1637 1638 1647] *See Fugitives, Liv. com: Tryalls.*

*(margin)* If taken after fff' it the value.

*(margin)* Strangers allowed by whom, and where.

*(margin)* How towns & perfons finable for entertaint

*(margin)* monthly forfeit. Conft: duty.

### Summons.

IT is ordered, and by this Court declared; that no *Summons,* Pleading, Judgement or any kinde of proceeding in Court or courfe of juftice fhall be abated, arefted or reverfed upon any kinde of circumftantial errors or miftakes, if the perfon and the Caufe be rightly underftood and intended by the Court.

2 And that in all cafes where the firft *Summons* are not ferved fix dayes before the Court, and the Cafe briefly fpecified in the *Warrant* where appearance is to be made by the partie fummoned; it fhall be at his libertie whether he will appear, or not, except all Cafes that are to be handled in Courts fuddenly called upon extraordinarie occafions. And that in all cafes where there appears prefent and urgent caufe any Affiftant or Officer appointed fhall have power to make out Attachments for the firft *Summons.* Alfo, it is declared that the day of *Summons* or Attachment ferved, and the day of appearance fhall be taken inclufively as part of the fix dayes. [1641 1647] *fee Prefidents.*

*(margin)* Circuftant: errors not prejudice Six days allowed the Defendant.

*(margin)* Provifo.

*(margin)* Where, & by whom Attachments graunted &c:

### Suits, vexatious fuits.

IT is ordered and decreed, and by this Court declared; that in all Cafes where it appears to the Court that the Plaintiffe hath willingly & wittingly done wrong to the Defendant in commencing and profecuting any Action, Suit, Complaint or Indictment in his own name or in the name of others, he fhall pay treble damages to the partie greived, and be fined fourty fhillings to the Common Treafurie. [1641 1646]

*(margin)* Treble dam: & Fine.

### Swyne.

IT is ordered by this Court, and by the Authoritie therof; that everie *Townfhip* within this Jurifdiction fhall henceforth have power, and are heerby required from time to time to make Orders for preventing all harms by fwine in corn, meadow, paftures and gardens; as alfo to impofe penalties according to their beft difcretion: and to appoint one of their Inhabitants by *Warrant* under the hands of the Select-men, or the Conftable where no Select-men are, to levie all fuch Fines and Penalties by them in that cafe impofed (if the Town neglect it).

And where Towns border each upon other, whofe Orders may be various, fatisfaction fhall be made according to the Orders of that Town where the damage is done.

But if the fwine be fufficiently ringed and yoaked, as the Orders of the Town to which they belong doth require, then where no fence is, or that it be infufficient through which the fwine come to trefpaffe, the Owner of the land or fence fhall bear all damages.

*(margin)* Town make orders.

*(margin)* impofe pena: levie them.

*(margin)* Orders of neight: towns various, yoaked &c:

*(margin)* infufficient fence.

G 3                                                                And

And if any swine be impounded for damage done as aforesaid, & there be kept three dayes, and that no person will own them; then the partie damnified shall give notice to the two next Towns (where any are within five miles compasse) that such swine are to be sold, by an out-crie, within three dayes next after such notice by the partie damnified; and in case none will buy, he shall cause them to be apprized by two indifferent men (one wherof shall be the Constable, or one chosen by him) signified under their hands in writing, and may keep them to his own use. And in both cases if the Owner shall after appear, the overplus according to valuation as afore-said (all damages and charges being payd) shall forthwith be rendred to him. And if any Town shall neglect to take order for preventing harms by swine according to this Law, more then one month after due publication heerof, such town shall forfeit to the Treasurie fourty shillings for everie month so neglecting, to be levied by the Marshal by *Warrant* from the Treasurer, upon due conviction before any Court or Magistrate, and signified to the Treasurer from time to time. [1647]

### Tile-earth.

IT is ordered by the Authoritie of this Court; that all *Tile-earth* to make sale ware shall be digged before the first of the ninth month, and turned over in the last, & first month ensuing, a month before it be wrought upon pain of forfeiting one half part of all such *tiles* as shal be otherwise made, to the use of the Common treasurie. [1646]

### Tobacco.

THIS Court finding that since the repealing of the former Laws against Tobacco, the same is more abused then before doth therfore order,

That no man shall take any *tobacco* within twenty poles of any house, or so neer as may indanger the same, or neer any Barn, corn, or hay-cock as may occasion the syring therof, upon pain of ten shillings for everie such offence, besides full recompence of all damages done by means therof. Nor shall any take *tobacco* in any Inne or common Victualing-house, except in a private room there, so as neither the Master of the said house nor any other Guests there shall take offence therat, which if any doe, then such person shall forthwith forbear, upon pain of two shillings sixpence for everie such offence. And for all Fines incurred by this Law, one half part shall be to the Informer the other to the poor of the town where the offence is done. [1638 1647]

### Torture.

IT is ordered, decreed, and by this Court declared; that no man shall be forced by torture to confesse any crime against himselfe or any other, unles it be in some Capital case, where he is first fully convicted by clear and sufficient evidence to be guilty. After which, if the Case be of that nature that it is very apparent there be other Conspirators or Confoederates with him; then he may be tortured, yet not with such tortures as be barbarous and inhumane.

2 And that no man shal be beaten with above fourty stripes for one Fact at one time. Nor shall any man be punished with whipping, except he have not otherwise to answer the Law, unles his crime be very shamefull, and his course of life vitious and profligate. [1641]

### Townships.

IT is ordered, decreed, and by this Court declared, that if any man shall behave himselfe offensively at any Town-meeting, the rest then present shall have power to sentēce him for such offence, so be it the *mulct* or penalty exceed not twēty shillings.

2 And that the Freemen of everie *Township*, and others authorized by law, shall have power to make such Laws and Constitutions as may concern the welfare of their Town. Provided they be not of a criminal but only of a prudential nature, and that their penalties exceed not twenty shillings (as aforesaid) for one offence, and that they be not repugnant to the publick Laws and Orders of the Countrie. And if any Inhabitant shall neglect or refuse to observe them, they shall have power to levie the appointed penalties by *distresse*.

3 Also that the Freemē of everie town or *Township*, with such other the Inhabitāts as have

have taken the Oath of fidelitie shall have full power to choos yearly, or for lesse time, within each *Township* a convenient number of fit men to order the planting and *prudential* occasions of that Town, according to instructions given them in writing.

Provided, nothing be done by them contrary to the publick Laws and Orders of the Countrie. Provided also that the number of such Select persons be not aboue nine.

4 Farther, it is ordered by the Authoritie aforesayd, that all Towns shall take care from time to time to order and dispose of all single persons, and In-mates within their Towns to service, or otherwise. And if any be grieved at such order or dispose, they have libertie to appeal to the next County Court.

5 *This Court taking into consideration the usefull Parts and abilities of divers Inhabitants amongst us, which are not Freemen, which if improved to publick use, the affairs of this Common-wealth may be the easier caried an end in the severall Towns of this Iurisdiction doth order, and heerby declare;*

That henceforth it shall and may be lawfull for the Freemen within any of the said Towns, to make choice of such Inhabitants (though non-Freemen) who have taken, or shall take the Oath of fidelitie to this Government to be Jurie-men, and to have their Vote in the choise of the Select-men for the town Affairs, *Assessements* of Rates, and other *Prudentials* proper to the Select-men of the severall Towns. Provided still that the major part of all companyes of Select-men be Free-men from time to time that shall make any valid Act. As also, where no Select-men are, to have their Vote in ordering of Schools, hearding of cattle, laying out of High-wayes and distributing of Lands; any Law, Use or Custom to the contrary notwithstanding. Provided also that no non-Freeman shall have his Vote, untill he have attained the age of twenty one years. [1636 1641 1647] *See Ecclesiast: Freeman, High-wayes.*

### Treasure.

IT is ordered, decreed and by this Court declared; that the general or publick Treasure, or any part therof shall never be expended but by the appointment of a General Court, nor any Shire treasure but by the appointment of the Freemen therof, nor any Town treasure but by the Freemen of that *Township*; except small sums upon urgent occasion, when the Court or the Freemen cannot direct therin, provided a just account be given therof. [1641]

### Tresspasse.

IT is ordered, decreed, and by this Court declared; that in all trespasses, or damages done to any man or men, if it can be proved to be done by the meer default of him or them to whom the trespasse is done, it shall be judged no trespasse, nor any damage given for it. [1641] *See Punishment.*

### Tryalls.

WHERAS this Court is often taken up in hearing and deciding particular Cases, between partie and partie, which more properly belong to other inferiour Courts, it is therfore ordered, and heerby declared,

That henceforth all Causes between partie and partie shall first be tryed in some inferiour Court. And that if the partie against whom the Judgment shall passe shall have any new evidence, or other new matter to plead, he may desire a new *Tryall* in the same Court upon a *Bill* of review. And if justice shall not be done him upon that *Tryall* he may then come to this Court for releif. [1642] *See Causes, Juries.*

2 It is ordered, and by this Court declared, that in all Actions of Law it shall be the libertie of the Plaintiffe and Defendant by mutuall consent to choos whether they will be tryed by the Bench or a Jurie, unles it be where the Law upon just reason hath otherwise determined. The like libertie shall be graunted to all persons in any criminal Cases.

3 Also it shall be in the libertie both of Plaintiffe and Defendant, & likewise everie delinquent to be judged by a Jurie, to challenge any of the Jurors, & if the challenge be found just and reasonable, by the Bench or the rest of the Jurie as the Challenger shall choos, it shall be allowed him, & *tales de circumstantibus* impannelled in their room.

4 Also

Select Townsmen their power in writing &c not aboue nine.

Single persons In-mates.

Non-Freemē chosen to office in Towns.

Caution.

Caution.

Publick Treasure

Town Treasure.

No Cause between partys come first to ſ Geu: Court Review

publ: liberty for tryals

& of deling: in criminals:

Challenges

*tales de circumstant.-bus*

**4** Also, children, Ideots, distracted persons and all that are strangers or new comers to our Plantation shall have such allowances, and dispensations in any Case, whether criminal or others, as Religion and reason require . [1641]

### Votes.

IT is ordered, decreed and by this Court declared ; that all, and everie Freeman, and others authorized by Law , called to give any Advice, Vote, Verdict or Sentence in any Court, Council or civil Assemblie , shall have full freedom to doe it according to their true judgements and consciences , so it be done orderly and inoffensively, for the manner . And that in all cases wherin any Freeman or other is to give his Vote be it in point of Election, making Constitutiõs and Orders or passing Sentence in any case of Judicature or the like , if he cannot see light or reason to give it positively, one way or other , he shall have libertie to be silent , and not pressed to a determinate vote . And farther that whensoever any thing is to be put to vote , and Sentence to be pronounced or any other matter to be proposed, or read in any Court or Assemblie, if the President or Moderator shall refuse to perform it, the major part of the members of that Court or Assemblie shall have power to appoint any other meet man of them to doe it . And if there be just cause, to punish him that should, and would not . [1641] See *Age* , *Townships Sect.* **5**.

### Vsurie .

IT is ordered, decreed & by this Court declared , that no man shall be adjudged for the meer forbearance of any debt, above eight pounds in the hundred for one year , and not above that rate proportionably for all sums whatsoever, *bills of Exchange* excepted , neither shall this be a colour or countenance to allow any *vsurie* amongst us contrary to the Law of God . [1641 1643]

### Watching.

FOR the better keeping Watches and Wards by the Constables in time of peace , it is ordered by this Court and Authoritie therof ;

That everie Constable shall present to one of the next Magistrates the name of everie person who shall upon lawfull warning refuse, or neglect to watch or ward, either in person, or by some other sufficient for that service . And if being convented, he cannot give a just excuse , such Magistrate shall graunt *Warrant* to any Constable to levie five shillings of such offender for everie such default ; the same to be imployed for the use of the Watch of the same Town . And it is the intent of the Law that everie person of able body (not exempted by Law) or of estate sufficient to hire another shall be lyable to watch and ward , or to supplye it by some other when they shall be therunto required . And if there be in the same house divers such persons , whether sons, servants or sojourners , they shall all be compellable to watch as aforesaid .

Provided that all such as keep families at their Farms , being remote from any Town, shall not be compellable to send their servants or sons from their Farms to watch and ward in the Towns . [1636 1646] See *Constables* , *Militarie* :

### Weights & Measures.

TO the end measures and weights may be one and the same throughout this Jurisdiction ; it is ordered by the Authoritie of this Court ,

That within one month after publication heerof the Auditor general shall provide upon the Countries charg such weights and measures, of all sorts as are heerafter expressed , for continuall Standards to be sealed with the Countrie Seal *viz.* one *Bushell*, one *Half-bushell* , one *Peck* and one *Half-peck* , one *Ale-quart* , one *Wine-pinte* and *Half-pinte* , one *Ell* and one *Yard* : as also a Set of brasse weights to four pounds, which shall be after sixteen *ounces* to the *Pound* , with fit *Skoaus* and *Steel-beams* to weigh and trye withall .

**2** And it is farther ordered by the Authoritie aforesaid , that the Constable of everie Town within this Jurisdiction shall within three months after publication heerof provide upon the Towns charge all such *Weights* , at the least of *Lad* , or such like ; and also sufficient *Measures* as are above expressed , tryed and sized by the Countries Standards.

---

*Marginal notes (left column):*

Infants, Ideots, strangers, like libertie

Freedom of votes & Caution.

liberty to be silent or neuter

where the Presid: will not put to vote.

Const: present defaults to § next Magistrate. Fin: 5 shil: to the use of the watch.

Who are compellable to watch

Auditor gen: to provide a Standard

Const: duty

Standards, and ſealed by the ſayd Auditor general, or his Deputie in his preſence (which ſhall be kept and uſed only for Standards for their ſeverall towns) who is heerby autho- rized to doe the ſame ; for which he ſhall receive from the Conſtable of each town, two pence for everie *weight* and *meaſure* ſo proved, ſized and ſealed . And the ſaid Conſtables of everie town ſhall commit theſe *weights* and *meaſures* unto the cuſtodie of the Select-men of their towns, for the time being, who with the ſaid Conſtable are heerby injoyned to chooſ out of their company one able man to be the Sealer of ſuch things for their town from time to time , and till another be choſen : which man, ſo choſen, they ſhall preſent to the next County Court there to be ſworn to the faithfull diſcharge of his duty , who ſhall have power to ſend forth his *Warrants* by the Con- ſtables to all the Inhabitants of their town to bring in all ſuch *meaſures* and *weights* as they make any uſe of , in the ſecond month from year to year , at ſuch time and place as he ſhall appoint , and make return to the Sealer in writing of all perſons ſo ſummoned that then and there all ſuch *weights* and *meaſures* may be proved and ſealed with the towns Seal (ſuch as in the Order for town cattle) provided by the Conſtable of each towns charge ; who ſhall have for everie *weight* and *meaſure* ſo ſealed, one pennie from the Owners therof at the firſt ſealing .

And all ſuch *meaſures* and *weights* as cannot be brought to their juſt Standard he ſhall deface, or deſtroy ; and after the firſt ſealing ſhall have nothing ſo long as they continue juſt with the Standard . And that none may neglect their duty therin, it is farther ordered by the Authoritie aforeſaid , that if any Conſtable, Select-men or Sealer doe not execute this Order, as to everie of them appertains , they ſhall forfeit to the common Treaſurie ſourty ſhillings for everie ſuch neglect the ſpace of one month : and alſo that everie perſon neglecting to bring in their *weights* and *meaſures* at the time and place appointed , they ſhall pay three ſhillings four pence for everie ſuch default , one half part wherof ſhall be to the Sealer, and the other half to the common Treaſurie, which the Sealer ſhall have power to levie by *diſtreſſe* from time to time . [1647]

### Wharfage.

I T is ordered by this Court and the Authoritie therof ; that theſe Orders ſhall be obſerved by all ſuch as ſhall bring goods to any *Wharf*, and theſe rates follow- ing be allowed ; firſt, for wood by the tun three pence , for timber by the tun four pence , for pipeſtaves by the thouſand nine pence , for boards by the thouſand ſix pence. For Merchants goods, whether in caſk or otherwiſe, by the tun ſix pence ; for drie fiſh by the *Quintall* one pennie , for corn by the quarter one pennie and a half pennie , for great cattle by the head two pence , for Goats, Swine or other ſmall cattle, except ſuch as are ſucking upon the dams, by the head a half-pennie : for hay, ſtraw and all ſuch combuſtable goods by the load ſix pence . For ſtones by the tun one pennie , for cot- ten wool by the bag two pence , for ſugar by the cheſt three pence . Provided that *Wharfage* be taken only where the *Wharfs* are made and maintained . And that wood, ſtone and weighty goods ſhall be ſet up an end , or layd ſeven foot from the ſide of the *Wharf*, upon penalty of double *Wharfage*, and ſo for other goods . And that no goods lye upon the *Wharf* above ſourtie eight hours, without farther agreement with the *Wharfinger* : and that it ſhall be lawful for the *Wharfinger* to take according to theſe rates out of the goods that are landed , except they be ſatiſied otherwiſe .

2 And it is farther ordered, that none ſhall caſt an Anker, Graplin or Killack within, or neer the Cove, where it may indanger any other veſſels, upon penaltie of ten ſhillings half to the Countrie, half to the *Wharfinger* beſides paying all damages .

3 And that it ſhall not be lawfull for any perſon to caſt any dung , draught, dirt, or any thing to fill up the Cove, or to annoy the neighbours, upon penaltie of ſourty ſhil- lings, the one half to the Countrie, and the other half to the *Wharfinger* . [1647]

### Wills inteſtate.

I T is ordered, and by this Court declared ; that when Parents dye *inteſtate*, he eldeſt ſon ſhall have a double portion of his whole eſtate reall, and perſonall unles the General Court upon juſt cauſe alledged ſhall judge otherwiſe . And when Parents

H      dye

---

*Marginal notes:*

his Fee, two pence.

Conſt: and Select-men appoint a Sealer . to be ſworn ƴ next County Court, his power & duty.

his Fee, one pennie.

What meaſ: deſtroyed, No Fees.

Rates for wharfage.

Wharfs made & maintain: orderly plac- ing goods.

caſt: Ankers, pen: 10 ſ. & damages,

caſt: dung &c: penal: 40 ſ.

dye *inteslate* having no Heirs males of their bodyes, their daughters shall inherit as co-partners, unles the General Court upon just reason shall judge otherwise. [1641]

*Witnesses.*

IT is ordered, decreed, and by this Court declared, that no man shall be put to death without the testimonie of two or three *witnesses*, or that which is equivalent therunto. [164·]

2 And it is ordered by this Court and the Authoritie therof, that any one Magistrate, or Commissioner authorized therunto by the General Court may take the Testimonie of any person of fourteen years of age, or above, of found understanding and reputation, in any Case civil or criminal; and shall keep the same in his own hands till the Court, or deliver it to the Recorder, publick Notarie or Clerk of the writs to be recorded, that so nothing may be altered in it. Provided, that where any such *witnesse* shall have his abode within ten miles of the Court, and there living and not disabled by sicknes, or other infirmitie, the said Testimonie so taken out of Court shall not be received, or made use of in the Court, except the *witnes* be also present to be farther examined about it. Provided also, that in all capital cases all *witnesses* shall be present wheresoever they dwell.

3 And it is farther ordered by the Authoritie aforesaid, that any person summoned to appear as a *witnes* in any civil Court between partie and partie, shall not be compellable to travell to any Court or place where he is to give his Testimonie, except he who shall so summon him shall lay down or give him satisfaction for his travell and expences, outward and home-ward; and for such time as he shall spend in attendance in such case when he is at such Court or place, the Court shall award due recompence. And it is ordered that two shillings a day shall be accounted due satisfaction to any *Witnes* for travell and expences: and that when the *Witnes* dwelleth within three miles, and is not at charge to passe over any other Ferrie then betwixt *Charlstown* and *Boston* then one shilling six pence *per diem* shall be accounted sufficient. And if any *Witnes* after such payment or satisfaction shall fail to appear to give his Testimonie he shall be lyable to pay the parties damages upon an action of the Case. And all *Witnesse* in criminal cases shall have suitable satisfaction, payd by the Treasurer upon *Warrant* from the Court or Judge before whom the case is tryed. And for a general rule to be observed in all criminal causes, both where the Fines are put *in certain*, and also where they are otherwise, it is farther ordered by the Authoritie aforesayd, that the charges of *Witnesses* in all such cases shall be borne by the parties delinquent, and shall be added to the Fines imposed; that so the Treasurer having upon *Warrant* from the Court or other Judge satisfied such *Witnesses*, it may be repayd him with the Fine: that so the *Witnesses* may be timely satisfied, and the countrie not damnified. [1647]

*Wolves.*

WHERAS great losse & damage doth befall this Common-wealth by reason of Wolves which destroy great numbers of our cattle notwithstanding provision formerly made by this Court for suppressing of them: therfore for the better incouragement of any to set about a work of so great concernment, it is ordered by this Court and Authoritie therof;

That any person either English or Indian that shall kill any *wolfe* or *wolves* within ten miles of any Plantation in this jurisdiction, shall have for everie *wolfe* by him or them so killed ten shillings payd out of the Treasurie of the Countrie. Provided that due proof be made therof unto the Plantation next adjoyning where such *wolfe* or *wolves* were killed: and also they bring a *Certificat* under some Magistrates hand, or the Constable of that place unto the Treasurer. Provided also that this Order doth intend only such Plantations as do contribute with us to publick charges, and for such Plantations upon the river of *Piscataway* that do not joyn with us to carie on publick charges they shall make payment upon their own charge. [1645]

*Wood.*

FOR the avoyding of injuries by carts and boats, to sellers and buyers of wood, it is ordered by this Court and the Authoritie therof,

That

---

Testimonie taken before one Magist:

how ordered:

Where witnis is to appear in person.

Capital cases.

charges of witnesses in civil cases to be layd down

Allowance to witnesses by the day.

Witnes not appearing pay damages.

witnes in criminal cases payd by the Treasurer, levied of ye delinquents

That where wood is brought to any town or house, by boat, it shall be thus accounted and assized. A boat of four tuns shall be accounted three loads; twelve tun nine loads, twenty tun fifteen loads. Six tun four load and half, fourteen tun ten load and half, twenty-four tun eighteen load. Eight tun six load, sixteen tun twelve load, twenty eight tun twenty one load. Ten tun seven load and half, eighteen tun thirteen load and half; thirty tun twenty two load and half. Except such wood as shall be sold by the *Cord*, which is, and is heerby declared to be eight foot in length, four foot in height, and four soot broad. [1646 1647]

### Workmen

BECAUSE the harvest of hay, corn, hemp and flax comes usually so neer together that much losse can hardly be avoyded, it is therefore ordered by the Authoritie of this Court;

That the Constables of everie town, upon request made to them, shal require any artificers or handy-crafts-men meet to labour, to work by the day for their neighbours in mowing, reaping of corn and inning therof. Provided that those men whom they work for shall duly pay them for their work. And that if any person so required shall refuse, or the Constable neglect his Office heerin, they shall each of them pay to the use of the poor of the town double so much as such dayes work comes unto. Provided no artificer or handy-crafts-man shall be compelled to work as aforesaid, for others, whiles he is necessarily attending on the like busines of his own. [1646]

### Wrecks of the sea

IT is ordered, decreed and by this Court declared; that if any ships or other vessels, be it freind or enemie, shall suffer ship-wreck upon our Coasts, there shall be no violence or wrong offered to their persons, or goods; but their persons shall be harboured and releived, and their goods preserved in safety, till Authoritie may be certified, and shall take farther order therin. Also, any Whale, or such like great fish, cast upon any shore shall be safely kept, or improved where it cannot be kept, by the town or other proprietor of the land; till the General Court shall set order for the same. [1641 1647]

---

### Presidents and Forms of things frequently used.

TO (*I B*) Carpenter, of (*D*). You are required to appear at the next Court, holden at (*D*) on the    day of the    month next ensuing; to answer the complaint of (*N C*) for with-holding a debt of    due, upon a *Bond* or *Bill*: or for two heifers &c: sold you by him, or for work, or for a trespasse done him in his corn or hay, by your cattle, or for a slaunder you have done him in his name, or for striking him, or the like, and heerof you are not to fail at your peril. Dated the   day of the   month 1641.

Summons.

TO the Marshal or Constable of (*B*) or to their Deputie. You are required to attach the body and goods of (*W I*) and to take *Bond* of him, to the value of    with sufficient Suertie or Suerties for his appearance at the next Court, holden at (*S*) on the   day of the   month; then, and there to answer to the complaint of (*I M*) for &c: *as before*. And so make a true return therof under your hand. Dated the   day &c:                                    *By the Court.*
                                                  R F.

Attach-ment.

KNOW all men by these presents, that wee (*A B*) of (*D*) Yeoman, and (*C C*) of the same, Carpenter, doe binde our selves, our Heirs and Executors to (*R F*) Marshal, or *M O* Constable of *D* aforesaid, in    pounds; upon condition that the

Bond for appearance

H a                                     said

said *A B* shall personally appear at the next Court, at *S* to answer *L M* in an Action
of   And to abide the order of the Court therin, & not to depart without licence.

**Replevin**

TO the Marshal or Constable of      You are required to *replevin* three heifers
of *T T* now distreined or impounded by *A B*, and to deliver them to the said
*T P*. Provided he give *Bona* to the value of   with sufficient Suertie or Sureties to
prosecute his *replevin* at the next Court, holden at (*b*) and so from Court to Court till
the Cause be ended, and to pay such costs and damages as the said ( *A B* ) shall by law
recover against him; and so make a true return therof under your hand. Dated &c.

by the Court.<br>R F.

**Commissio-
ners for the
united
Colonies.**

WHERAS upon serious consideration, wee have concluded a confœderacie with the
english Colonies of *New-Plimouth*, *Conecticot* and *New-Haven*, as the bond of
nature, reason, Religion and respect to our Nation doth require.

Wee have this Court chosen our trustie and well-beloved freinds (*S I* ) and (*W T*)
for this Colonie, for a full and compleat year, as any occasions and exigents may require;
and particularly for the next Meeting at (*b*). And do invest them with full power and

**their power**

authoritie to treat, and conclude of all things, according to the true tenour and meaning
of the Articles of confœderation of the united Colonies, concluded at *Boston* the
ninth day of the third month 1643.

**Oath of
fidelitie.**

I (*A B*) being by Gods providence an Inhabitant within the Jurisdiction of this
Common wealth, doe freely and sincerly acknowledge my selfe to be subject to
the Government therof. And doe heer swear by the great and dreadfull Name of the
Ever-living God, that I will be true and faithfull to the same, and will accordingly yeild
assistance therunto, with my person and estate, as in equitie I am bound: and will also
truly indeavour to maintein and preserve all the Liberties & Priviledges therof, submitting my self unto the wholsom Laws made, & established by the same. And farther,
that I will not plot or practice any evil against it, or consent to any that shall so doe:
but will timely discover and reveal the same to lawfull Authoritie now heer established,
for the speedy preventing therof. So help me God in our Lord Jesus Christ.

**Freemans
Oath.**

I (*A B*) being by Gods providence an Inhabitant within the Jurisdiction of this
Common-wealth, and now to be made free; doe heer freely acknowledge my
self to be subject to the Government therof: and therefore do heer swear by the great
and dreadfull Name of the Ever-living God, that I will be true and faithfull to the same,
& will accordingly yeild assistance & support therunto, with my person and estate, as in
equitie I am bound, and will also truly indeavour to maintein & preserve all the Liberties and Priviledges therof, submitting my self unto the wholsom Laws made and established by the same. And farther, that I will not plot or practice any evil against it,
or consent to any that shall so doe; but will timely discover & reveal the same to lawfull authoritie now heer established, for the speedy prevention therof.

Moreover, I do solemnly binde my self in the sight of God, that when I shall be
called to give my voice touching any such matter of this State, wherin Free-men are to
deal; I will give my vote and *suffrage* as I shall in mine own conscience judge best to
conduce and tend to the publick weal of the Body, without respect of persons, or favour of any man. So help me God &c.

**Governours
Oath.**

WHERAS you (*J W* ) are chosen to the place of a Governour over this Jurisdiction, for this year, and till a new be chosen & sworn: you do heer swear by
the Living God, that you will in all things concerning your place, according to your
best power and skill carie and demean your self for the said time of your Government,
according to the Laws of God, & for the advancement of his Gospell, the Laws of this
Land, and the good of the people of this Jurisdiction. You shall doe justice to all men
without partialitie, as much as in you lyeth: you shall not exceed the limitations of a
Governour in your place. So help you God &c:

**Deputie
Gover:**

WHERAS you (*T L*) are chosen to the place of the Deputie-Governour &c:
as in the Governours Oath, *mutatis mutandis*.

a H                            Wheras

WHERAS you (R B) are chosen to the place of *Assistant* over this Jurisdiction, for this year, and till new be chosen and sworn: you doe heer swear by the Living God, that you will trulie indeavour according to your best skill, to carie and demean your self in your place, for the said time, according to the Laws of God & of this land, for the advancement of the Gospell & the good of the people of this Jurisdiction. You shall dispense justice equallie and impartiallie, according to your best skill in all cases wherin you shall act by vertue of your place. You shall not wittinglie & willinglie exceed the limitations of your place. And all this to be understood, during your abode in this jurisdiction. So help you God in our Lord Jesus Christ.

WHERAS you (E) have been chosen to the Office of Sergeant Major General, of all the militarie Forces of this Jurisdiction, for this present year: You doe heer swear by the Ever-living God, that by your best skill and abilitie you will faithfullie discharge the trust committed to you, according to the tenour and purport of the Commission given you by this Court. So help you God &c:

I (R I) being chosen *Treasurer* for the Jurisdiction of the *Massachusets*, for this year, and untill a new be chosen; doe promise to give out *Warrants* with all convenient diligence, for collecting all such sums of monie as by any Court, or otherwise have been, or shall be appointed, and to pay out the same, by such sums and in such manner as I shall be lawfullie appointed by this Court, if I shall have it in my hands of the Common Treasurie. And will return the names of such Constables as shall be failing in their Office, in not collecting and bringing in to mee such sums as I shall give *Warrant* for. And will render a true account of all things concerning my said Office, when by the General Court I shall be called thereto. So help me God in our Lord Jesus Christ.

YOu (W H) heer swear by the Name of the Living God; that in the Office of a *Publick Notarie*, to which you have been chosen, you shall demean your selfe diligentlie and faithfullie according to the dutie of your Office. And in all writings, instruments & articles that you are to give testimonie unto, when you shall be required, you shall perform the same trulie and sinceerlie according to the nature therof, without delay or *covin*. And you shall enter, and keep a true Register of all such things as belong to your Office. So help &c:

YOu (E M) shall diligentlie, faithfullie, and with what speed you may, collect and gather up all such Fees, and sums of monie, in such goods, as you can finde, of everie person for which you shall have *Warrant* so to do by the Treasurer for the time being. And with like faithfullnes, speed and diligence levie the goods of everie person for which you shall have *Warrant* so to doe, by vertue of any *Execution* graunted by the Secretarie, or other Clerk authorized therunto, for the time being. And the same goods so collected or levied, you shall with all convenient speed deliver in to the Treasurer, or the persons to whom the same shall belong. And you shall with like care & faithfullnes, serve all *Attachments* directed to you, which shall come to your hands; & return the same to the Court where they are returnable, at the times of the return therof. And you shall perform, doe and execute all such lawfull commands, directions and warrants, as by lawfull Authoritie heer established shall be committed to your care & charge, according to your Office. All these things in the presence of the Living God you binde your selfe unto, by this your Oath to perform, during all the time you continue in your Office, without favour, fear, or partialitie of any person. (And if you meet with anie case of dificultie which you cannot resolve by your selfe, you may suspend till you may have advice from Authoritie) So help &c:

YOu (N D) do swear by the Living God, that you will well and trulie serve this Common-wealth in the Office of *Auditor General*, wherunto you have been chosen; so long as you shall continue in the same. You shall keep a true account of all things committed to your charge. You shall not omit or delay without just occasion, to examin, signe and dispatch all accounts and bills which shall be brought to you for that end, without taking any Fee or reward for the same, other then the

General Court hath allowed, or shall allow : and shall give a true account of all your busines, when you shall be thereto required by the said Court. So help you God &c:

**Associates.**

YOU (*M A*) being chosen Associate for the Court, for this year, and till new be chosen or other order taken, doe heer swear, that you will doe equal right and justice in all cases that shall come before you, after your best skill and knowledge, according to the laws heer established. So help you God &c:

*Wheresoever any three men are deputed to end small Causes, the Constable of the place within one month after, shall return their names to the next Magistrate, who shall give Summons for them forthwith to appear before him; who shall administer to them this Oath:*

**Three men.**

YOu (*A B*) being chosen & appointed to end small Causes, not exceeding fourty shillings value, according to the laws of this Jurisdiction, for this year ensuing, doe heer swear by the Living God that without favour or affection, according to your best light, you will true Judgement give and make, in all the Causes that come before you. So help you God &c:

**Grand Iurie.**

YOu swear by the Living God, that you will diligently inquire, & faithfully present to this Court, whatsoever you know to be a breach of any law established in this Jurisdiction according to the minde of God ; and whatsoever criminal offences yon apprehend fit to be heer presented, unles some necessary and religiousitye of conscience, truly grounded upon the word of God binde you to secresie. And whatsoever shall be legally committed by this Court to your judgement, you will return a true and just Verdict therin, according to the evidence given you, and the laws established amongst us. So help you God &c:

**Pettie Iurie.**

YOu swear by the Living God, that in the Cause or Causes now legally to be committed to you by this Court, you will true triall make, and just verdict give therin, according to the evidence given you, and the laws of this Jurisdiction. So help you God &c:

**Life & death.**

YOu doe swear by the great Name of Almightie God, that you will well & truly trie, and true deliverance make of such prisoners at the Bar as you shall have in charge, according to your evidence. So help you God &c:

**Witnesses.**

YOu swear by the Living God, that the evidence you shall give to this Court concerning the Cause now in question, shall be the truth, the whole truth, and nothing but the truth. So help you God &c:

**Untimely death.**

YOu swear by the Living God, that you will truly present the cause and the manner of the death of (*Y B*) according to evidence, or the light of your knowledge and conscience. So help you God &c:

*The form of the Oath to be administred to the Sergeant Majors of the severall Regiments, and so,* mutatis mutandis, *to the other militarie Officers.*

**Sergeant Major & other chief Officers.**

WHeras you (*R S*) have been chosen to the Office of Sergeant Major, of the Regiment in the Countie of *M.* for this present year, and untill another be chosen in your place ; You doe heer swear by the Living God, that by your best skill & abilitie you will faithfully discharge the trust committed to you, according to such commands and directions as you shall from time to time upon all occasions receive from the Sergeant Major General, by vertue of his Commission from the Court, and according to the Laws and Orders by this Court made and established in this behalf. So help you God &c:

**Clerk of the Band.**

YOu (*R. B*) swear trulie to perform the Office of a Clerk of a trained Band, to the utmost of your abilitie, or indeavours, according to the particulars specified [and peculiar to your office] in the militarie Laws. So help &c:

**Commissio: of martial disciplin**

YOu shall faithfullie indeavour with all good conscience, to discharge this trust committed to yon, as you shall apprehend to conduce most to the safetie of this Common-wealth. You shall not by any sinister devices, or for any partial respects, or private ends doe any thing to the hindrance of the effects of any good and seasonable Counsels. You shall appoint or remove no Officer by anie partialitie, or for personal respects, or other prejudice : but according to the merit

merit of the persons in your apprehentions. You shall faithfully indeavour to see that martial disciplin may be strictly upholden, not easing or burthening any, otherwise then you shall judge to be just and equal. You shall use your power over mens lives, as the last and only means which in your best apprehentions shall be most for the publick safety in such case. So help you God in our Lord Jesus Christ.

WHERAS you (*E G*) are chosen Constable within the Town of (*C*), for one year now following, and untill other be sworn in the place: you doe heer swear by the Name of Almighty God, that you will carefully intend the preservation of the peace, the discovery and preventing all attempts against the same. You shall duly execute all *Warrants* which shall be sent unto you from lawfull Authoritie heer established, & shall faithfully execute all such Orders of Court as are committed to your care: and in all these things you shall deal seriously and faithfully while you shall be in office, without any sinister respects of favour or displeasure, So help you God &c:

WHERAS you (*J G*) are chosen an Officer for the searching and sealing of leather within the Town where you now dwell, for the space of a year, and till another be chosen and sworn in your room. You do heer swear by the Ever-living God, that you will carefully and duly attend the execution of your said Office, with all faithfullnes for the good of the Common-wealth, according to the true intent of the Laws in such case provided. So help you God &c:

YOU (*C D*) heer swear by the Living God that you will from time to time faithfully execute your Office of *Clerk of the Market*, in the limits whereto you are appointed, for this ensuing year, and till another be chosen and sworn in your place: and that you will doe therin impartially, according to the Laws heer established, in all things to which your Office hath relation. So help you God &c:

YOU (*S S*) doe heer swear by the Ever-living God, that you will to your power faithfully execute the Office of a *Searcher* for this year ensuing, and till another be chosen and sworn in your place, concerning all goods prohibited; and in special, for *Gun-powder, Shot, Lead and Amunition*: and that you will diligently search all vessels, carriages and persons that you shall know, suspect, or be informed are about to transport, or carie the same out of this Jurisdiction contrary to Law. And that you will impartially seiz, take, and keep the same in your own custodie: one half part wherof shall be for your service in the said Place; the other you shall forthwith deliver to the Treasurer. All which goods so seized and disposed, you shall certifie under your hand to the Auditor-general within one month from time to time. So help you God &c:

WHERAS you (*T. D.*) are chosen *Apprizers* of such *lands* or goods as are now to be presented to you, you doe heer swear by the Living-God, that all partialitie, prejudice and other sinister respects layd aside, you shall apprize the same, and everie part therof, according to the true and just value therof at this present, by common account, by your best judgement and conscience. So help you God &c:

WHERAS you (*J. B.*) are chosen to be *Viewers of Pipe-staves* within the Town of (*B*) you doe heer swear by the Ever-living God, that at all convenient times while you shall be in place, when you shall be required to execute your Office, you shall diligently attend the same; and shall faithfully without any sinister respects, try and sort all *Pipe-staves* presented to you, and make a true entrie therof according to law. So help you God in our Lord Jesus Christ.

## FINIS

# List of Entries and Sources of "Laws"

The following table to all the entries in the *Lawes and Libertyes* provides the page reference in the facsimile for each entry. It also indicates the source of each entry, or the sections of each entry, provided the source could be found in either the published records of the General Court or in the "Body of Liberties" of 1641. If the source was not found or if the "law" was a matter of established practice, such is noted. Differences between the source and the "law" are also indicated.

The first column gives the page reference in the facsimile.

The second column gives the title of the "law" as it appears in the facsimile.

The third column indicates the clause or section of an entry (if it is divided). Section numbers assigned by the editor for purposes of clarity are in [ ]. "P" stands for the preamble (if any) to the provision, if it has a separate source.

The date of the source is given in the fourth column. For the "Body of Liberties" this is merely "1641." In a few instances a date will appear in " " indicating that the source of the "law" though not found was so dated at the end of the entry in the *Lawes and Libertyes*. All dates are based on the new year beginning on 1 January.

If the source is found in the *Records of the Governor and Company of the Massachusetts Bay*, volume 1 (1628-41) or volume 2 (1642-49), N. B. Shurtleff, ed. (Boston, 1853), the appropriate volume/page reference is given under the heading "Mass. Rec."

Where a specific source could not be found, one of the following symbols will be found in the column under "Mass.Rec.":

EP=Established practice (a footnote will instance the practice).

NF=Not found, in either "Mass.Rec." or the "Body of Liberties." *Records of the Governor and Company of the Massachusetts Bay*, N. B. Shurtleff,

ed., volume 3 (Boston, 1854), the records of the Deputies in the General Court for 1644-57, has been searched for missing sources of "laws," without success.

If the source of the "law" is found in the "Body of Liberties" of 1641, the clause number of the "Liberty" is given under the heading "Body/Lib," and refers to the facsimile and transcription printed in *The Colonial Laws of Massachusetts*, W. H. Whitmore, ed. (Boston, 1889).

Any difference between the "law" and the source is indicated in the next to the last column on the right in the table:

0=No change, or virtually no change; changes only in unimportant wording.

1=Significant change in wording, quantities, figures, elements, etc.

2=Change in the entire construction of the entry.

Where the only change in the "law" is a matter of a changed jurisdiction occasioned by the increasing sophistication of the courts in Massachusetts, this is considered as "0" difference. The last category, "2," indicates that the difference is so considerable that the source is at best tenuously related to the "law."

Where two or more sources have been conflated, this is indicated by bracketing and a "C."

The last column indicates the nature of the difference between the source and the "law":

A=Additional material in the "law."

D=Deletion of a considerable proportion of the original provision.

R=Rearrangement of the provisions in the source.

No attempt has been made to determine the sources for the "Presidents and Forms of Things Frequently Used" appended in the *Lawes and Libertyes*. Most of the oaths of office, etc., can be found in the published records of the General Court.

| Page | Title | Cl. | Date | Mass.Rec. | Body/Lib | Diff. | Nature |
|---|---|---|---|---|---|---|---|
| 1 | [Preamble and first clause: express law, etc., provision] | P | 1641 | | Preamble | o | |
| | | [1] | 1641 | | 1 | o | |
| | Abilitie. | | 1641 | | 11 | o | |
| | Actions. | [1] | 14 June 1642 | 2:16 | | o | |
| | | 2 | 27 Sept 1642 | 2:28 | | 1 | A |
| | | 3 | 11 Nov 1647 | 2:215 | | o | |
| | | 4 | 1641 | | 28 | o | |
| | Age. | | 1641 | | 53 | o } | C D |
| | | | 11 Nov 1647 | 2:204 | | 2 } | |
| | Ana-Baptists. | P | 13 Nov 1644 | 2:85 | | o | |
| 2 | | [1] | 13 Nov 1644 | 2:85 | | 1 | D |
| | Appeale. | [1] | 1641 | | 36 | 1 } C | D |
| | | | 11 Nov 1647 | 2:219 | | 2 } | A/D |
| | | 2 | 1642 | 2:3 | | o | |
| | Appearance, Non-apearance. | | 1641 | | 4 | o | |
| | Arrests. | | 1641 | | 33 | o } | |
| | | | 6 Sept 1638 | 1:239 | | 2 } C | |
| | | | 11 Nov 1647 | 2:204 | | 2 } | |
| 3 | Attachments. | | 12 Nov 1644 | 2:80 | | o | |
| | Bakers. | | 4 Nov 1646 | 2:181 | | 1 } C | D |
| | | | | EP [Clerk market][1] | | | |
| | Ballast. | [1] | 7 Dec 1636 | 1:185 | | o | |
| | | 2 | 7 Sept 1643 | 2:44 | | o | |
| | Barratrie. | | 1641 | | 34 | 1 | A |
| 4 | Benevolence. | | 2 June 1641 | 1:327 | | 1 | D |
| | Bills. | | 16 Aug 1631 | 1:90 | | 2 | A |
| | Bond-slavery. | | 1641 | | 91 | o | |
| | Bounds of Townes and Persons. | P | 11 Nov 1647 | 2:210 | | o | |
| | | [1] | 11 Nov 1647 | 2:210 | | o | |
| | | [2] | 11 Nov 1647 | 2:210 | | o | |
| | Burglarie and Theft. | P | | NF | | | |
| | | [1] | 14 June 1642 | 2:22 | | 1 } C | A/D |
| | | | "1647" | NF [first offence][2] | | | |
| 5 | | 2 | 4 Nov 1646 | 2:180 (s654) | | o } | |
| | | | 26 May 1647 | 2:192 | | o } C | |
| | | | 4 Nov 1646 | 2:180 (s652) | | o } | |
| | CAPITAL LAWES. | [1]-2 | 1641 | | 94 (1-2) | o | |
| | | 3 | 1641 | | 94 (3) | o } C | |
| | | | 4 Nov 1646 | 2:176 | | o } | |
| | | 4-7 | 1641 | | 94 (4-7) | o | |
| | | 8 | 1641 | | 94 (8) | o } C | |
| | | | | NF [under aet.14] | | | |

| Page | Title | Cl. | Date | | Mass.Rec. | Body/Lib | Diff. | Nature |
|---|---|---|---|---|---|---|---|---|
| 6 | | 9-12 | | 1641 | | 94 (9-12) | 0 | |
| | | 13 | 4 Nov | 1646 | 2:179 | | 0 | |
| | | 14 | 4 Nov | 1646 | 2:179 | | 1 | D |
| | | 15 | 14 Jan | 1642 | 2:21 | | 0 | |
| | Cask & Cooper. | | 27 Sept | 1642 | 2:21 | | 0 } | C |
| | | | | "1647" | NF [gagers app'tment] | | | |
| | Cattel. Corn-fields. Fences. | [1] | 20 Nov | 1637 | 1:215 | | 0 | |
| | | 2 | 17 Oct | 1643 | 2:49 | | 2 } | C A/D |
| | | | 26 May | 1647 | 2:195 | | 2 | D |
| | | 3 | 26 May | 1647 | 2:190 | | 0 } | C |
| | | | 14 June | 1642 | 2:15 | | 0 | |
| 7 | | 4 | 9 Mar | 1637 | 1:189 | | 0 | |
| | | 5 | 26 May | 1647 | 2:195 | | 0 | |
| | | 6 | | "1647" | NF | | | |
| 8 | | 7 | | | NF [unfenced lands] | | | |
| | | | 14 June | 1642 | 2:15 | | 2 } | C A/D |
| | | | 20 Nov | 1637 | 1:215 | | 2 | A/D |
| | Causes. Small Causes. | [1] | 6 Sept | 1638 | 1:239 | | 2 | A/D |
| | | | 10 Dec | 1641 | 1:344 | | 2 } | C |
| | | | 14 June | 1642 | 2:16 | | 1 | D |
| | | [2] | 11 Nov | 1647 | 2:209 | | 2 | A |
| | | | 2 Oct | 1646 | 2:162 | | 2 } | C A/D |
| | | | 11 Nov | 1647 | 1:209 | | 0 | |
| 9 | Charges publick. | [1] | | 1641 | | 63 | 1 } | C A |
| | | | 3 Sept | 1635 | 1:159 | | 2 | D |
| | | 2 | 3 Sept | 1634 | 1:124 | | 0 | |
| | | 3 | 6 Sept | 1638 | 1:240 | | 0 } | C D |
| | | | 7 Mar | 1644 | 2:60 | | 1 | |
| | | 4 | 11 Nov | 1647 | 2:212 | | 1 | D |
| 10 | | | 2 June | 1641 | 1:330 | | 0 } | C |
| | | | 5 Nov | 1639 | 1:277 | | 0 | |
| 11 | Children. | [1] | 14 June | 1642 | 2:8 | | 2 | D |
| | | 2 | 11 Nov | 1647 | 2:217 | | 0 | |
| 12 | | 3 | | 1641 | | 83 | 0 | |
| | | 4 | | 1641 | | 84 | 1 } | C D |
| | | | | "1646" | NF [woman's minority] | | | |
| | Clerk of writs. | | 10 Dec | 1641 | 1:344 | | 0 | |
| | Colledge. | P | | | NF | | | |
| | | [1] | 27 Sept | 1642 | 2:30 | | 0 | |
| | Condemned. | | | 1641 | | 44 | 0 | |
| 13 | Constables. | [1] | 7 Oct | 1641 | 1:339 | | 0 | |
| | | 2 | | | NF [convey. prisoners] | | | C D |
| | | | 4 Nov | 1646 | 2:182 | | 2 } | |
| | | 3 | 6 May | 1646 | 2:150 | | 0 } | C |
| | | | 4 Nov | 1646 | 2:182 | | 0 | |
| | Conveyances fraudulent. | [1] | | 1641 | | 15 | 0 | |
| | | 2 | 7 Oct | 1640 | 1:306 | | 1 | A/D |

| Page | Title | Cl. | Date | Mass.Rec. | Body/Lib | Diff. | Nature |
|------|-------|-----|------|-----------|----------|-------|--------|
| 14 | Councill. | | 12 Aug 1645 | 2:125 | | o | |
| | Courts. | [1] | 3 Mar 1636 | 1:169 [Qtr. Crts] | | o | |
| | | | 3 Mar 1636 | 1:169 [Boston] | | 2 | |
| | | | 25 May 1636 | 1:175 | | 1 | |
| | | | 3 Mar 1636 | 1:169 [Essex] | | 1 | |
| | | | 25 May 1636 | 1:175 | | 1 | C |
| 15 | | | 2 June 1641 | 1:325 [Salem] | | o | |
| | | | [14] Mar 1648 | 2:227 [Middlesex] | | 1 | A |
| | | | [14] Mar 1648 | 2:227 [Norfolk] | | 1 | D |
| | | | 10 May 1648 | 2:242 | | 1 | D |
| | | | 3 Mar 1636 | 1:169 | | 1 | |
| | | | | NF [priority/divorce][3] | | | |
| | | 2 | 6 June 1639 | 1:264[4] | | 1 | A/D |
| | | 3 | 5 Nov 1639 | 1:277 | | o | |
| | | | 11 Nov 1647 | 2:219 | | 2 | C |
| 16 | | 4 | 7 Mar 1644 | 2:58 | | 1 | A |
| | Criminal causes. | | 1641 | | 41 | o | |
| | Crueltie. | | 1641 | | 92 | o | |
| | Damages pretended. | | 1641 | | 22 | o | |
| | Death untimely. | | 1641 | | 57 | o | |
| | Deeds and writings. | | 1641 | | 40 | o | |
| | Deputies for the Generall Court. | P | | NF | | | |
| | | [1] | 14 May 1634 | 1:118 | | 1 | D |
| 17 | | 2 | 8 Sept 1636 | 1:178 | | 2 | D |
| | | | 13 Mar 1639 | 1:254 | | o | C |
| | | | | NF [with next town] | | | |
| | | 3 | 4 Mar 1635 | 1:142 | | o | |
| | | | 3 Sept 1635 | 1:157 | | o | C |
| | | 4 | 1641 | | 62 | 1 | C D |
| | | | 1641 | | 68 | 1 | D |
| | Distresse. | | 1641 | | 35 | o | |
| | Dowries. | | "1647" | NF[5] | | | |
| 18 | Drovers. | | 1641 | | 93 | o | |
| | Ecclesiasticall. | 1 | 1641 | | 95 (1) | o | |
| | | | 3 Mar 1636 | 1:168 | | o | C |
| | | 2 | 3 Mar 1636 | 1:168 | | o | |
| | | 3 | 1641 | | 95 (2) | o | |
| | | 4 | 1641 | | 95 (3) | o | |
| | | 5 | 1641 | | 95 (4) | o | |
| | | 6 | 1641 | | 95 (5) | o | |
| | | 7 | 1641 | | 95 (6) | o | |
| | | 8 | 1641 | | 95 (7) | o | |
| | | 9 | 1641 | | 95 (8) | o | |
| 19 | | 10 | 1641 | | 95 (9) | o | |
| | | 11 | 1641 | | 95 (10) | o | |
| | | 12 | 1641 | | 95 (11) | o | |
| | | 13 | 4 Nov 1646 | 2:179 | | 1 | |

| Page | Title | Cl. | Date | | | Mass.Rec. | Body/Lib | Diff. | Nature |
|------|-------|-----|------|---|---|-----------|----------|-------|--------|
| 20 | | 14 | 4 Nov | 1646 | | 2:178<br>NF [one magistrate]6 | | o⎫<br> ⎬ C | |
| | | 15 | 3 Mar | 1636 | | 1:168 | | 2⎫ | |
| | | | | 1641 | | | 58 | o⎬ C | |
| | | | | 1641 | | | 59 | o | |
| | | | | 1641 | | | 60 | o⎭ | |
| | | 16 | 11 Nov | 1647 | | 2:209 | | o⎫<br> ⎬ C | |
| | | | 11 Nov | 1647 | | 2:217 | | o⎭ | |
| | Elections. | [1] | 7 Sept | 1643 | | 2:42 | | o⎫<br> ⎬ C | |
| | | | 17 Oct | 1643 | | 2:48 | | o⎭ | |
| | | 2 | 11 Nov | 1647 | | 2:220 | | o | |
| 21 | | 3 | 11 Nov | 1647 | | 2:210 | | 1 | R |
| | | 4 | | 1641 | | | 67 | o | |
| | Escheats. | | 4 Nov | 1646 | | 2:182 | | o | |
| | Fayrs & Markets. | | 4 Mar | 1634 | | 1:112 [Boston] | | o⎫ | |
| | | | 3 Sept | 1634 | | 1:127 [Salem] | | o | |
| | | | 4 Nov | 1646 | | 2:164 [Lynn] | | o | |
| | | | 9 Mar | 1637 | | 1:189 [Charlestown] | | o⎬ C | |
| | | | 6 Sept | 1638 | | 1:241 [Salem] | | o | |
| | | | 6 Sept | 1638 | | 1:241 [Watertown] | | o | |
| | | | 6 Sept | 1638 | | 1:241 [Dorchester] | | o⎭ | |
| 22 | Ferrie. | [1] | 7 Oct | 1641 | | 1:338 | | o⎫ | |
| | | | 7 Oct | 1641 | | 1:341 | | o | |
| | | | 22 May | 1646 | | 2:154 | | o⎬ C | |
| | | | 13 Nov | 1644 | | 2:84 | | o | |
| | | | 22 May | 1646 | | 2:154 | | 1⎭ | |
| | | [2] | 4 Nov | 1646 | | 2:170 | | o | |
| | Fines. | | 6 Sept | 1638 | | 1:239 | | 1 | |
| | Fyre. | | 4 Nov | 1646 | | 2:180 | | 1⎫ | A |
| | | | 5 Nov | 1639 | | 1:281 | | 2⎬ | C A/D |
| | | | 4 Nov | 1646 | | 2:180 | | o⎭ | |
| 23 | Fish. Fisher-men. | | 6 May | 1646 | | 2:147 | | o | |
| | Forgerie. | | 4 Nov | 1646 | | 2:181 | | o | |
| | Fornication. | | 14 June | 1642 | | 2:21 | | 1 | |
| | Freemen, Non-Freemen. | | 11 Nov | 1647 | | 2:208 | | o | |
| | Fugitives, Strangers. | | | 1641 | | | 89 | o | |
| 24 | Gaming. | | 26 May | 1647 | | 2:195 | | o⎫ | |
| | | | 4 Nov | 1646 | | 2:180 | | o⎬ C | |
| | | | 26 May | 1647 | | 2:195 | | o⎭ | |
| | Generall Court. | [1] | | 1641 | | | 72 | o | |
| | | [2] | | 1641 | | | 73 | o | |
| | | [3] | | 1641 | | | 69 | o | |
| | Governour. | | | 1641 | | | 71 | o | |
| | Heresie. | | 4 Nov | 1646 | | 2:1777 | | 1 | A/D |
| | Hydes & Skins. | | 4 Nov | 1646 | | 2:168 | | 1 | A/D |
| 25 | Hygh-wayes. | [1] | 5 Nov | 1639 | | 1:280 | | o | |
| | | 2 | [May] | 1642 | | 2:4 | | 1 | A |
| | | 3 | 26 May | 1647 | | 2:192 | | 1⎫<br> ⎬ C | A |
| | | | 5 Nov | 1639 | | 1:280 | | o⎭ | |
| | Idlenes. | | 1 Oct | 1633 | | 1:109 | | o | |

| Page | Title | Cl. | Date | Mass.Rec. | Body/Lib | Diff. | Nature |
|---|---|---|---|---|---|---|---|
| 26 | Jesuits. | | 26 May 1647 | 2:193 | | o | |
| | Impost. | [1] | 11 Nov 1647 | 2:224 | | o | C |
| | | | 11 Nov 1647 | 2:225 | | o | |
| 27 | | 2 | 10 May 1648 | 2:246 | | o | |
| 28 | Impresses. | | 1641 | | 5 | o | |
| | | | 1641 | | 6 | o | C |
| | | | 1641 | | 7 | o | |
| | | | 1641 | | 8 | o | |
| | Imprisonment. | | 1641 | | 18 | o | |
| | Indians. | [1] | 4 Mar 1634 | 1:112 | | 2 | A |
| | | | 17 May 1637 | 1:196 | | o | C |
| | | | 15 Nov 1637 | 1:209 | | o | |
| | | 2 | 14 June 1642 | 2:16 | | 1 | D |
| | | 3 | 13 May 1640 | 1:294 | | 1 | A |
| | | | NF [fencing] | | | | C |
| | | | NF [cattle injury] | | | | |
| 29 | | 4 | 4 Nov 1646 | 2:178 | | o | C |
| | | | 4 Nov 1646 | 2:177 | | o | |
| | Inditements. | | 4 Nov 1646 | 2:182 | | o | |
| | In-keepers, Tippling, Drunkenes.8 | P | | NF | | | |
| 30 | | [1] | 14 May 1645 | 2:100 | | 1 | A |
| | | [2] | | NF [sign] | | | C |
| | | | 14 May 1645 | 2:100 | | 1 | A |
| | | [3-4] | 14 May 1645 | 2:100 | | 1 | C D |
| | | | 4 Nov 1646 | 2:172 | | 1 | D |
| | | [5] | 14 May 1645 | 2:100 | | 1 | C D |
| | | | 4 Nov 1646 | 2:172 | | 1 | D |
| | | [6] | 4 Nov 1646 | 2:172 | | o | |
| | | [7] | 14 May 1645 | 2:100 | | o | |
| | | [8] | 4 Nov 1646 | 2:172 | | o | |
| | | [9] | 14 May 1646 | 2:100 | | 1 | A |
| 31 | | [10] | | NF [profit] | | | |
| | | | 11 Nov 1647 | 2:215 | | o | C |
| | | | EP [accounting]9 | | | | |
| | | | 11 Nov 1647 | 2:215 | | o | |
| | | [11] | | NF | | | |
| | | [12] | | NF | | | |
| | | [12-13] | 4 Nov 1646 | 2:172 | | 1 | A/D |
| | | [14] | 6 May 1646 | 2:150 | | 1 | D |
| | | | 4 Nov 1646 | 2:171 | | 1 | C D |
| | | | 20 Nov 1637 | 1:214 | | 1 | A |
| | | | NF | | | | |
| | Iuries, Iurors. | [1] | 14 May 1634 | 1:118 | | 1 | A |
| | | | NF [process] | | | | C |
| | | | 14 June 1642 | 2:21 | | o | |

| Page | Title | Cl. | Date | Mass.Rec. | Body/Lib | Diff. | Nature |
|---|---|---|---|---|---|---|---|
| 32 |  | 2 | 14 May 1634 | 1:118 |  | o |  |
|  |  | 3 | 4 Mar 1635 | 1:143 |  | 1 } | C A |
|  |  |  | 1641 |  | 31 | o } |  |
|  |  | 4 |  | NF[10] |  |  |  |
|  |  | 5 |  | 1641 | 76 | o |  |
|  |  |  |  | 1641 | 49 | o } | C |
|  |  |  |  | NF [life & death] |  |  |  |
|  | Iustice. |  | 1641 |  | 2 | o |  |
|  | Lands, Free lands. |  | 1641 |  | 10 | 1 | A |
|  | Leather. | P-[7] | 14 June 1642 | 2:18 |  | o |  |
| 33 |  | [8] | 14 June 1642 | 2:18 |  | 1 } | C A/D |
|  |  |  | 27 Sept 1642 | 2:31 |  | o } |  |
|  |  | [9-10] | 14 June 1642 | 2:18[11] |  | o |  |
| 34 |  | [11] | 11 Nov 1647 | 2:216 |  | o |  |
|  |  | [12] | 14 June 1642 | 2:20 |  | o } | C |
|  |  |  | 27 Sept 1642 | 2:31 |  | o } |  |
|  | Levies. |  | 11 Nov 1647 | 2:204 |  | o |  |
| 35 | Liberties Common. | [1] | 1641 |  | 12 | o |  |
|  |  | 2 | 1641 |  | 16 | o } | C |
|  |  |  | "1647" | NF [tidal property][12] |  |  |  |
|  |  | 3 | 1641 |  | 17 | o } |  |
|  | Lying. |  | 14 May 1645 | 2:104 |  | 1 | A |
| 36 | Magistrates. | P-[1] | 20 Nov 1637 | 1:212 |  | o } | C D |
|  |  |  | 1641 |  | 20[13] | 1 } |  |
|  |  | 2 | 1641 |  | 19 | 1 |  |
|  |  | 3 | 12 Aug 1645 | 2:215 |  | 2 | D |
|  |  | 4 | 3 Mar 1636 | 1:170 |  | o |  |
|  |  | 5 | 10 May 1643 | 2:39 |  | o |  |
| 37 | Man-slaughter. |  | 11 Nov 1647 | 2:212[14] |  | 1 | D |
|  | Marriage. | [1] | 9 Sept 1639 | 1:275 |  | o |  |
|  |  | 2 | 11 Nov 1647 | 2:207 |  | o |  |
|  |  | 3 | 11 Nov 1647 | 2:211 |  | o |  |
| 38 |  | 4 |  | EP[15] |  |  |  |
|  | Marshal. |  | 22 May 1646 | 2:153 |  | 1 | A/D |
|  | Masters, Servants, Labourers. | [1] | 28 Sept 1630 | 1:76 |  | o |  |
|  |  | 2 | 1 Oct 1633 | 1:109 |  | o |  |
|  |  | 3 | 3 Sept 1635 | 1:157 |  | o |  |
|  |  | 4 | 28 Oct 1636 | 1:183 |  | o |  |
|  |  | 5 | 7 Oct 1641 | 1:340 |  | 1 | D |
| 39 |  | 6 | 1641 |  | 85 | o |  |
|  |  | 7 | 1641 |  | 86 | 1 | A |
|  |  | 8 | 1641 |  | 87 | o |  |
|  |  | 9 | 1641 |  | 88 | o |  |
|  | Militarie Affairs. | P |  | NF |  |  |  |

| Page | Title | Cl. | Date | | Mass.Rec. | Body/Lib | Diff. | Nature |
|---|---|---|---|---|---|---|---|---|
| 40 | | [1]-3 | 14 May | 1645 | 2:117 | | 1 | A/D |
| | | 4 | 14 May | 1645 | 2:120 | | 0 | |
| 41-42 | | 5-16 | 11 Nov | 1647 | 2:221 | | 0 } C | |
| | | | 11 Nov | 1647 | 2:216 | | 0 } | |
| 43 | | 17 | 11 Nov | 1647 | 2:224 | | 1 | A |
| | Mills, Millers. | | 3 Mar | 1636 | 1:168 | | 0 } C | |
| | | | 6 Sept | 1638 | 1:241 | | 1 } | D |
| | Monopolies. | | | 1641 | | 9 | 0 | |
| | Oaths, Subscription. | | | 1641 | | 3 | 0 } C | |
| | | | [May] | 1642 | 2:4 | | 0 } | |
| | Oppression. | | 3 Sept | 1635 | 1:160 | | 0 | |
| | Payments. | | 7 Oct | 1640 | 1:304 [16] | | 2 } C | D |
| | | | | | NF [proviso] | | | |
| 44 | Pipe-staves. | | 4 Nov | 1646 | 2:169 | | 0 | |
| | Poor. | | 6 June | 1639 | 1:264 | | 0 | |
| | Pound, Pound breach. | [1] | 8 July | 1635 | 1:150 | | 1 } C | A/D |
| | | | 11 Nov | 1647 | 2:220 | | 1 } | A/D |
| 45 | | 2 | 11 Nov | 1647 | 2:220 [17] | | 2 | D/R |
| | Powder. | | 1 Oct | 1645 | 2:136 | | 0 | |
| | Prescriptions. | | | 1641 | | 65 | 0 | |
| | Prisoners, Prisons. | | 4 Nov | 1646 | 2:182 | | 0 | |
| | Profane swearing. | | 4 Nov | 1646 | 2:178 | | 0 | |
| | Protestation contra Remonstrance. | | | 1641 | | 75 | 0 | |
| 46 | Punishment. | | | 1641 | | 42 | 0 } C | |
| | | | | 1641 | | 46 | 0 } | |
| | Rates, Fines. | | 7 Oct | 1640 | 1:302 | | 1 | D |
| | Records. | P-[1] | 9 Sept | 1639 | 1:275 | | 1 } C | D |
| | | | 11 Nov | 1647 | 2:208 | | 1 } | D/R |
| | | 2 | 11 Nov | 1647 | 2:208 | | 0 | |
| | | 3 | 14 June | 1642 | 2:15 | | 1 | |
| | | 4 | 7 Mar | 1644 | 2:59 | | 0 | |
| 47 | | 5 | | 1641 | | 38 | 1 | D |
| | | | | 1641 | | 48 | 0 } C | |
| | | | | 1641 | | 64 | 0 } | |
| | Replevin. | | | 1641 | | 32 | 0 | |
| | Schools. | | 11 Nov | 1647 | 2:203 | | 0 | |
| | Secresie. | | | 1641 | | 61 | 0 | |
| | Secretarie. | | | "1647" | EP [18] | | | |
| 48 | Ships, Ship-masters. | [1] | 7 Oct | 1641 | 1:337 | | 1 | A |
| | | 2 | 14 May | 1645 | 2:109 | | 0 | |
| | Straies. | [1] | 20 Nov | 1637 | 1:211 | | 1 | |
| | | | 14 June | 1642 | 2:14 | | 1 } C | A |
| | | | | | NF [above 20s.] | | | |
| | | [2] | | | NF [no notice] | | | |
| | | | 5 Nov | 1639 | 1:281 | | 1 } C | D |
| | | | | | NF [no owner] | | | |
| | | [3] | | | NF [proviso] | | | |

| Page | Title | Cl. | Date | Mass.Rec. | Body/Lib | Diff. | Nature |
|---|---|---|---|---|---|---|---|
| 49 | Strangers. | | 17 May 1637 | 1:196 | | I | } C D |
| | | | 6 Sept 1638 | 1:241 | | I | |
| | Summons. | [1] | 1641 | | 25 | o | |
| | | 2 | 1641 | | 21 | o | } C |
| | | | 26 May 1647 | 2:194 | | o | |
| | Suits, vexatious suits. | | 1641 | | 37 | I | } C A D |
| | | | 4 Nov 1647 | 2:181 | | I | |
| | Swyne. | | 11 Nov 1647 | 2:220 | | o | |
| 50 | Tile-earth. | | 4 Nov 1646 | 2:180 | | o | |
| | Tobacco. | | 6 Sept 1638 | 1:241 | | I | D } C D |
| | | | 6 May 1646 | 2:151 | | I | |
| | | | | NF [informer] | | | |
| | Torture. | [1] | 1641 | | 45 | o | |
| | | 2 | 1641 | | 43 | o | |
| | Townships. | [1] | 1641 | | 56 | o | |
| | | 2 | 1641 | | 66 | o | |
| | | 3 | 1641 | | 74 | I | A |
| 51 | | 4 | 13 Dec 1636 | 1:186 | | o | |
| | | 5 | 26 May 1647 | 2:197 | | I | D |
| | Treasure. | | 1641 | | 78 | o | } C |
| | | | | NF [small sums] | | | |
| | Trespasse. | | 1641 | | 24 | o | |
| | Tryalls. | [1] | 14 June 1642 | 2:16 | | o | |
| | | 2 | 1641 | | 29 | o | |
| | | 3 | 1641 | | 30 | o | |
| 51 [sic., 52] | | 4 | 1641 | | 52 | o | |
| | Votes. | | 1641 | | 70 | o | |
| | | | 1641 | | 77 | o | } C |
| | | | 1641 | | 54 | o | |
| | Usurie. | | 1641 | | 23 | o | } C |
| | | | 17 Oct 1643 | 2:48 | | o | |
| | Watching. | [1] | 6 May 1646 | 2:151 | | o | |
| | | [2] | 9 Mar 1637 | 1:190 | | o | |
| | Weights & Measurers. | | 11 Nov 1647 | 2:211 | | o | |
| 53 | Wharfage.[19] | [1] | 4 Nov 1646 | 2:170 | | I | |
| | | 2 | | NF | | | |
| | | 3 | | NF | | | |
| | Wills intestate. | | 1641 | | 81 | o | } C |
| | | | 1641 | | 82 | o | |
| 54 | Witnesses. | [1] | 1641 | | 47 | o | |
| | | 2-3 | 11 Nov 1647 | 2:204 | | o | |
| | Wolves. | | 14 May 1645 | 2:103 | | o | |
| | Wood. | | | NF [preamble] | | | |
| | | | 4 Nov 1646 | 2:181 | | o | } C |
| | | | | NF [cord][20] | | | |

| Page | Title | Cl. | Date | | Mass.Rec. | Body/Lib | Diff. | Nature |
|------|-------|-----|------|--|-----------|----------|-------|--------|
| 55 | Workmen. | | 4 Nov 1646 | | 2:180 | | 0 | |
| | Wrecks of the sea. | | 1641 | | | 90 | 0 ⎫ | C A/D |
| | | | 18 Oct 1645 | | | | 2 ⎭ | |

PRESIDENTS and FORMS of
 THINGS FREQUENTLY
 USED.
Summons.
Attachment.
Bond for Appearance.

56 Replevin.
Commissioners for the united
 Colonies; their power.
Oath of fidelitie.
Freemans Oath.
Governours Oath.
Deputie Gover.[nor]

57 Assistants.
Major General.
Treasurer.
Publick Notarie.
Marshal.
Auditor General.

58 Associates.
Three men. [small causes]
Grand Iurie.
Pettie Iurie.
Life & Death. [jury]
Witnesses.
Untimely death. [jury]
Sergeant Major & other chief
 Officers.
Clerk of the Band.
Commissio[ners] of martial
 disciplin.

59 Constable.
Leather Sealer.
Clerk of the Market.
Searcher.
Apprizers.
Viewers of Pipestaves.

## NOTES TO LIST OF ENTRIES AND SOURCES OF "LAWS"

1 Two clerks of the market were appointed by the General Court at the time the general order of 4 November 1646 was promulgated, Mass. Rec. 2:181. However, appointment of clerks by each town to be sworn in county court, powers of entry, etc., extension to butter, and allowance of one-third of the forfeiture to the clerk appear to have become regular practice between 1646 and 1648 without explicit order for the same.

2 Punishment here prescribed for burglary (and house breaking) and robbery is considerably more specific and probably much more severe than that in the law of 14 June 1642, which provided that these offenses "bee severely punished, according to the nature of the offence, & the severall aggravations thereof, as the iudges shall appoint . . ." Mass. Rec. 2:22.

3 Priority in the Court of Assistants as set out in this "law" appears to have no specific authorization by the general orders of the General Court, though it made sense. The exclusive jurisdiction of Assistants in divorce is likewise without explicit provision found. However, the Governor, Council, and Assistants on 2 June 1636 heard the divorce case of Richard Beggarly and his wife; the Court of Assistants, 3 December 1639, annulled the second of James Luxford's two marriages; the Boston Quarter Court of Assistants, 5 March 1644, granted a divorce to Anne Clarke on the grounds of her husband's desertion, J. Noble ed., *Records of the Court of Assistants Massachusetts*, 2 (Boston, 1904), pp. 62 n, 89, 138.

4 This provision of 6 June 1639 was explicitly to continue no longer than the September 1640 session of the General Court. The order of 6 June 1639 has a marginal note against it, "Expired." There is no record of its having been extended at the 7 October 1640 session of the General Court (there was no September session).

5 "Body of Liberties," cl. 79, gave power to the General Court to provide relief for a widow who was not left a "competent portion" of her dead husband's estate. Otherwise, I have been unable to find provision for dowries, etc. On 2 May 1649, the General Court ordered an amendment in the "law" here set down by which the provision for one-third of the husband's estate to go to the widow was repealed. By the same order the "act or consent of such wife" was interpreted to mean a writing acknowledged before a magistrate to be a full bar, and in the case of intestacy the county court had power to assign to the widow and the children, "or other heires," portions of the deceased's personal estate, Mass. Rec. 2:281. In the House of Deputies, 4 May 1649, a two-man committee was appointed to draft a law for women's dowries, Mass. Rec. 3:154. Before the *Lawes and Libertyes* provision, the General Court, 26 May 1647, allowed a widow her husband's tools in recognition of her charges in educating their son to whom the husband's real property had been bequeathed; the son and a daughter were to have each only £9 from the personal estate, Mass. Rec. 2:194.

6 The power of one magistrate to hear and determine cases of non-attendance at church services was in keeping with the increasing devolution of jurisdiction in minor offenses to the magistrates.

7 The provision for banishment of heretics and "seducers" to heresy indicates a considerable hardening of attitude toward heresy between 4 November 1646, when this law was passed in General Court, and early 1648 when the *Lawes and Libertyes* went to press. The 1646 law provided that a heretic who did not recant was to be fined 20s. per month for the first six months and 40s. per month thereafter until he recanted; a "seducer" to heresy was to pay a fine of £5 for every offense.

8 The numerous provisions under this title for which no source can be found in the records of the General Court is very puzzling. The items are significant; it is difficult to believe that the committees for the laws undertook such large-scale additions without explicit confirmation by the General Court.

9 The requirement for a retailer of wine to account with the auditor-general appears to have been established practice. By general order of 1 October 1645, the "custome of wines shalbe left to the care of the auditor generall," Mass. Rec. 2:131. By general order of 6 May 1646, considerable powers of search and seizure of wines not entered with the auditor-general were given to the auditor-general with power to require the aid of constables and other officers in the search and seizure, Mass. Rec. 2:148.

10 The assumption of jurisdiction by the General Court of a case in which the bench and the jury could not "proceed with peace of conscience" is reasonable, but of such far-reaching procedural importance as to appear to have required explicit order or legislation by the General Court.

11 The provisions in law for search and seizure of defective leather of 14 June 1642 were given a definitive interpretation by the General Court upon the petition of the leather-searchers, 11 November 1647, Mass. Rec. 2:215.

12 The General Court on 17 October 1649 dealt with the question of town lands between "the salt marsh & the low water marke" growing out of the earliest foundations of towns in the colony, and referred to an earlier "order" of the General Court making "all the lands to low water marke to be the proprietors of the land joyning therevnto . . ." Mass. Rec. 2:284. I have not been able to find the "order" referred to.

13 Virtually nothing of the "Body of Liberties" provision (cl. 20) remains in this "law" save the last phrase of the second paragraph, "and censured at the next superiour Court." This is an unusual treatment of a provision in the "Body of Liberties," but the General Court's orders of 20 November 1637 (Mass. Rec. 2:212-13) were much more comprehensive than clause 20.

14 The deletions in this "law" from the original provision of 11 November 1647 consist of the high-flying preamble to the same—there being no provision against burglary and other "violent" assaults of persons and goods, especially travelers and inland (i.e., outlying) inhabitants by

Indians and others, etc.—and the terminal citation to Exodus 22:2. The common law's provision for justifiable homicide, especially *se defendendo*, was apparently more appropriate in the eyes of the committees for the laws than the Old Testament's "If a thief be found breaking up, and be smitten that he die, there shall no blood be shed for him."

15 There are a number of instances extant in the records of the General Court for the appointment of commissioners for marriage in settlements where no magistrate resided or was resident nearby. The earliest reference to these commissioners that I could find is in the general order of 14 June 1642 requiring the magistrates and "other persons appointed to marry" to deliver annually records, etc., to the recorder of the nearest court, Mass. Rec. 2:15.

16 The provision for payments in kind, of 7 October 1640, was expressly repealed by both houses of the General Court on 6 May 1646, Mass. Rec. 3:69 (Deputies' records), and henceforth all bargains made for money were to be paid in money. However, no entry of this order is to be found in the records of the upper house, the Governor and Assistants.

17 Under the original law of 11 November 1647, pound-breach was punishable by only ten stripes; in the "law" it is twenty. There is considerable rearrangement of the original in this "law."

18 This "law" appears to have been the work of the committees for the laws, but it was based on existing practice.

From 1635 the Secretary was elected by the court of elections of the General Court, although whether annually is not entirely clear until 1644 and after. On 17 October 1649, the General Court "commended to the seuerall tounes . . . whither the Secretary were not to be left to the Gennerall Courts choyce, whose honnor is principally concerned therein, then to be chosen by the people," and left it to the court of election of the next year to give the proposal a year's trial, Mass. Rec. 2:285.

19 The rates for wharfage in the general order of 4 November 1646 were generally lower than those in the "law"; in the latter, the rates are usually double. On 11 November 1647, wharfage rates were submitted to the examination of a three-man committee (none of whom were on the committee for the laws) who were to "returne what they iudge meete" to the next session of the court, Mass. Rec. 2:205. There is no further mention of their report or actions; we can assume that their work was, however, the basis for the increased rates in the *Lawes and Libertyes*. The provisions in clauses 2 and 3 for the prevention of casting anchors, etc., and of water pollution and filling coves might also have been the work of this committee.

20 A "cord" of wood has always been and still is defined as in this "law" throughout New England and Maritime Canada: 4' x 4' x 8' (128 cubic feet). This appears to have been long established (albeit with minor local variations) in England, R. E. Zupko, *A Dictionary of English Weights and Measures* (Madison, 1968) p. 42.